America's Cup Course is:
1st leg – to windward, or weather leg (Aussies sometimes call it a "work")
2nd leg – reach on starboard tack
3rd leg – reach on port tack
4th leg – windward (course can be moved if wind shifts)
5th leg – run (returning to A.C. buoy)
6th leg – windward

On windward leg 12 meter cannot sail directly into wind but must "tack" at angles about 40° from wind. This is where tactics come into play as each yacht tries to cover or to tack away from the other.

Cannot use spinnaker to windward only on reaches and run.

Wind

Windward or "weather" mark

Finish line

Committe yacht "Carltina" anchors after 5th leg

Starboard tack lay line (yacht on starboard tack can "fetch" mark)

Port tack lay line

26

4

Reaching on starboard tack

Reaching spinnaker

Running spinnaker

4

Running on port tack

Running on starboard tack

Reaching or "wing" mark

Mark boat

Windward yacht is ahead and has more wind (arrows represent wind)

Leeward yacht is "blanketed" – having less wind

Starboard tack has right of way

Port tack must keep clear

Windward yacht is "backwinded"

4

Yacht behind tries to blanket opponent

26

Wind is deflected (arrows) by leeward yacht

Tacking angle 100° to 105°

Starting line

Committee Yacht "Carltina" anchors for start

America's cup buoy

BHW

RACING FOR THE AMERICA'S CUP, 1974

THEODORE A. JONES
9/10/76

RACING FOR THE AMERICA'S CUP, 1974
THE VIEW FROM THE CANDY STORE
THEODORE A. JONES

Quadrangle ▮▮▮ The New York Times Book Co.

Library of Congress Cataloging in Publication Data
Jones, Theodore A
Racing for the America's Cup, 1974.

1. America's Cup races. 2. Yacht racing.
I. Title.
GV830 1974.J66   797.1′4   74–26009
ISBN 0–8129–0542–3

To Bob Harris
So that he might be there
after all

CONTENTS

Contents

ACKNOWLEDGMENTS

The author acknowledges the valuable assistance of Jack L. Spangler who kindly made his yacht *Gamecock* available at the height of the yachting season. Without *Gamecock* the view from The Candy Store would have been limited severely.

Lucia Carpenter's prowess as a typist, editor, critic, and transcriber of indecipherable tapes and notes is very evident to the author. Thanks to her expertise and hard work the complicated process of assembling a manuscript in a fearful hurry has gone without a hitch.

Jeff Hammond, Associate Editor of *Yachting*, and Mike Levitt, Associate Editor of *Yacht Racing*, contributed articles which are incorporated in the manuscript. Jeff's "The Script Changes at Newport" became Chapter 6, and Mike's photographs and interview with Judy Koch are a key part of Chapter 11.

Acknowledgments

The many people who are characterized herein are thanked for being themselves. Without them the view from The Candy Store would be much less interesting.

It should be evident that without the dedication of the crew members and the moral and financial support of the contributors to the several 12-Meter syndicates the America's Cup would cease to exist as an exciting spectacle and sporting event.

Without David Ray's Candy Store there would be no place to gather to talk about it all.

Ted Jones
November, 1974

INTRODUCTION: BARON BICH IN 1970

It was a foggy August evening in 1970 when Baron Marcel Bich, millionaire developer of the Bic pen, once dapper and arrogant in his white yachting attire, finally came down the dock. He was damp, bedraggled, and looked the part of a tired, beaten man. There was nothing he could say to ameliorate his decisive defeat at the hands of Australia's *Gretel II* and the humiliation that his *France*, which he had been unable to navigate in the fog, did not even cross the finish line in her last bid for the America's Cup.

    To appreciate what the man in rumpled white must have felt at that moment as he and his entourage moved out to face the public, one had to have been aware of the tremendous multimillion-dollar, three-year effort he had made to win the Cup and had to have seen him that morning as he took the helm. Having found fault with a procession of helmsmen all summer, "Monsieur le Baron" had dis-

charged his last skipper and taken command himself. Had he done so
quietly his situation would not have been quite so impossible, but he
had taken charge with his customary flourish, stepping aboard in a
completely white yachting outfit—shoes, trousers, jacket, cap, even
gloves—as if to declare to the world that he alone was capable of
saving the honor of France.

After the race, *France* had been hours late coming into the harbor. The whistles, sirens, and cheers for the victorious Aussies had
finally faded with the sunlight, and most of the spectators had gone
on to dinner and the night's celebrations. Had *France* waited until
dark to sneak into harbor and avoid the gaze of the spectators? Did
the Baron need to gain his composure before facing the public and
reporters? Whatever the reason, he was finally coming toward the
Newport Shipyard gate and approaching the battery of newspaper-
men, photographers, and television cameramen (and a handful of
spectators) anxious to capture the cocky Frenchman's reaction now
that three years of bombastic rhetoric had culminated in defeat.

Suddenly, the Baron's knot of people stopped. Voices were raised
in anger, curses in French. The crowd swayed toward the Baron in its
center. People ran. Flashbulbs exploded with light. Fists were raised.
Arms flailed. Someone fell. The crowd pulsated away from its center
and back again, shuffling and scuffling.

"What's happening?"

"What's going on?"

"Incroyable! Incroyable!"

Incredible indeed! Incredible that here in the elegant town of
Newport, amid these splendid surroundings reminiscent of genteel
times, here at this serious match in the world's most decorous sport
was a common fist fight! It was not just an ordinary fist fight, but
Monsieur le Baron himself had taken a poke at one of the French
television cameramen and knocked him down. It was said later that
the cameraman had pushed the Baron's wife.

Incredible indeed! It was here ashore, as well as on the race
course, that the America's Cup spectacle took place. The drama was
not only of muscle and machines, but also of human emotion wrung
to the breaking point.

It was perhaps this incident more than any other significant con-
frontations on the race course that summed up the essence of an
America's Cup summer, for it is more than just two yachts battling

for honor. It is all the things that go on in conjunction with the Cup
races. From the action at The Candy Store to the bachelor dormitories
of the Bellevue Avenue mansions, from the courtesy wagons piled
high with sailbags to the Cup Committee's yacht glistening with
varnish, from the polished bottom of a 12-Meter to its masthead wind
vane, from the crew's uniforms to the sweat and salt that stains them,
from outboards buzzing in the harbor to the thousand regal yachts
following the races offshore, from the long-haired young woman with
a guitar to the painted mannequin dining at The Black Pearl, from
the arguments in the Thames Street bars to the deliberations of the
International Jury—these are the things that make an America's Cup
summer a unique, spectacular sports event.

The best view is not only from the spectator fleet offshore. The
view is also from such vantage points as the outdoor bars at The
Black Pearl and The Candy Store.

The view from The Candy Store,
HMS Rose replica and Newport
Harbor.

"...from the long-haired young
woman with a guitar..."

RACING FOR THE AMERICA'S CUP, 1974

HELP!

**MONDAY,
SEPTEMBER 2**

"Coast Guard Cutter *Point Turner*, Coast Guard Cutter *Point Turner*, this is *Gamecock One*, Whiskey Hotel Zulu 9178, over."

"Station calling the *Point Turner*, this is *Point Turner*, go ahead."

"*Point Turner*, this is *Gamecock One*, switch to 2670."

"Roger, switching."

"*Gamecock*, this is *Point Turner* on 2670."

"Roger, *Point Turner*, this is *Gamecock One*. We are in the spectator fleet on the America's Cup course and have broken down in the vicinity of the finish line. We are at the finish mark and drifting onto the course with no engine. Can you get us off the course?"

"*Gamecock One*, *Point Turner*, the Coast Guard vessel 41321 will tow you off the course. Stay on this frequency."

"Thank you *Point Turner*. We'll look for 321. *Gamecock* out."

1

Thus, very embarrassed, I concluded a summer bouncing around the ocean in a 1948 vintage 38-foot powerboat riding the end of a towline back to Newport. *Gamecock* was my floating hotel, office, observation post, photography platform, and daily transportation nine, and more, miles out to sea. Now she was but a silent follower being greeted in the harbor by horns, whistles, and applause—not for *Gamecock*, but for *Intrepid* and *Courageous*, the latter having at that moment been named to defend the America's Cup.

We had watched the most exciting series of trial races in America's Cup history. We had also watched the Australian's 12-Meter *Southern Cross* beat Baron Bich's *France* in four straight races to win the right to challenge for the America's Cup, but now we had a week's respite in which to fix *Gamecock*'s engine, touch base with the office, have film developed, and repair cameras before the main event— *Courageous* defending against *Southern Cross* in what promised to be one of the best match races in the entire 123-year history of America's Cup competition.

A few days earlier, Red Smith, writing in *The New York Times*, had taken issue with the America's Cup as a sporting event. Smith's thesis was that the challenger never got a fair shake and that Australians in particular never got a fair shake in this country (citing the deaths of boxer Lee Darcy and race horse Phar Lap as examples of American inhospitality to Aussie challengers). Smith quoted Australia's Martin Visser, *Gretel II*'s starting helmsman when she was protested and disqualified from the second race in 1970, who had advocated an International Jury to decide protests. Smith wrote, "There is no international committee. There never has been." Smith's statement was incorrect. Partly because of criticism such as Visser's and partly because it made good sense to get itself off the hook, the New York Yacht Club had agreed to have an International Jury decide protests.

Smith was asked to retract his misstatement. He did, but in so doing leveled another blast at the America's Cup competition, claiming that it was a put-up job and that the world would have been better off if John Cox Stevens (who was interested in horse racing as well as yachting) had made his cup a challenge trophy for horses instead of boats.

Unfortunately, Red Smith's lack of enthusiasm for this symbolically important yachting event is typical of many sportswriters and much of the sports-page reading public as well. It probably stems from ignorance of the history of the America's Cup. If one views the competition out of its historical context it certainly does appear that the New York Yacht Club has been arbitrary and one-sided in its administration of the America's Cup. However, if one takes the trouble to understand what the competition represents and how it came about, it becomes clear that it is both important and unique in yachting history.

The America's Cup is two distinct contests—one the public sees and one the participants engage in. Owing to the technical nature of yacht racing, the general public is often ignorant of the nuances of tactics, sail trim, and concentration that comprise the effort. What appears from a distance to be idle motion to fans used to the "hut, hut, hut, pound, slam, thump" of a football scrimmage is in reality just as active and just as demanding mentally and almost as demanding

Gamecock rides placidly at her mooring, the skiff in her cockpit.

physically. What appears to be a graceful yacht lazing along in the gentle swells with only one person's head and shoulders standing sedately by the wheel is in reality a shell containing eleven men working to harness the unexpectedly strong forces required to propel a 12-Meter through the water. (At a normal speed of eight knots a 70,000-pound 12-Meter will thrust aside an equal weight of water every 3⅓ *seconds!*) That this effort is both physical and mental is not apparent to the casual observer. Nor is the precision with which each maneuver must be timed appreciated by the uninitiated. Thus, seeing no activity and little relative movement, was Ring Lardner inspired to make his famous and oft-quoted—yet completely irrelevant—remark that watching an America's Cup race was like watching grass grow. To those who understand the conflict of forces and wits that take place on a race course, the spectacle can be slow agony or heart-stopping excitement.

Yacht racing is a sport of efficiencies. An inch of adjustment on a genoa sheet, a quarter of a spoke of movement of the wheel, a second's indecision by the tactician, or a one-degree variation by the navigator can mean the difference between defeat and victory. A tack that is initiated a few seconds too early or too late can lose a race that takes hours to sail. Minuscule errors unsuspected by the inexperienced and sometimes even undetected by the experienced observer may take many minutes for their effect to be felt. All this time the crews are working with the utmost concentration to make their yacht sail fastest in the right direction. The aficionado senses the conflict and writhes in inner agony until the outcome is clear. The casual observer, unaware of the drama that is unfolding before him, yawns, takes another slug from his hip flask, and wonders who won the fifth race at Aqueduct.

At times things happen with such speed that the observer wonders if he really saw them. Such was the time in 1962 when *Gretel* passed *Weatherly* rounding the reaching mark of the second race. *Weatherly* appeared to have a comfortable lead when suddenly *Gretel* got up on a wave and surfed by with a great war whoop from her crew. *Weatherly*'s crew—who were wrestling with a broken spinnaker pole —like most of the spectators, didn't know what was happening until it was all over.

Similarly, at the start of the second race in 1970, *Intrepid* streaked in from outside the starting line and leaped between *Gretel*

II and the Committee boat to take the start with a maneuver so sudden that the Aussies fouled *Intrepid* while trying to recover their advantage. Many spectators failed to appreciate the developing situation, but knowledgeable observers were held spellbound for over a minute while the situation developed and then flashed to a climax. (That this is one of the most controversial moments in America's Cup history is largely because the action was so lightning fast that few observers were able to piece together what they had seen.)

Throughout its history, from its very origin, the America's Cup competition has been largely misunderstood and misinterpreted by the general public. The Ring Lardners and Red Smiths are partly responsible for this. Not that they can be blamed for their cynicism; who can be thrust into the middle of a complicated and subtle situation with no previous background in it and come up with sage advice? A little more knowledge of the history of the America's Cup would seem useful at this point.

In 1850 a syndicate headed by Commodore John Cox Stevens of the New York Yacht Club, commissioned the design and building of a yacht, which they intended to sail to England and race against English yachtsmen. Commodore Stevens was made to feel welcome through correspondence with Lord Wilton, Commodore of the Royal Yacht Squadron, and *America* arrived in England on July 31, 1851, from Le Havre, where she had been refitted after crossing the Atlantic on her own bottom.

Charles Boswell compiled considerable contemporary data on *America*'s challenge, which is reproduced in his history *The America*. It appears from these accounts that the general public was much more aware of the sport of yacht racing than it is today. Perhaps this was because the sport was relatively new and the exclusive plaything of the wealthy few, but it also may have been because the sailing vessel was much more a part of everyday life in 1851 than it is today. Whatever the reason, the arrival of *America* was well publicized in advance, and the outcome of her meeting with the *Lavrock*—a new, fast English yacht, which went out to meet her—was of great interest.

With an injudicious show of speed, *America*, pressed on by her owners, whipped the *Lavrock* soundly. Perhaps because they were as anxious as the English to see what the untried *America* could do, perhaps because they were caught up in their own zeal to win, whatever their reason, *America*'s owners pushed her so that she caught and passed *Lavrock* and beat her to Cowes by a third of a mile in the short space of four miles.* Since part of their reason for the voyage was to win money from English yachtsmen who thought their yachts were able to beat *America* and backed their convictions with substantial bets, this first trouncing of one of England's fastest yachts did nothing to make other English yachtsmen want to risk their purses and their yachts' reputations.

America languished at the Isle of Wight with no one willing to race against her. She did manage to enter a race run by the Royal Yacht Squadron's rival Royal Victoria Yacht Club in Ryde, I.O.W., but this club withdrew *America*'s entry by reason of her being owned by more than one person. *America* brushed with the contestants anyway and, according to contemporary reports, beat them all handily.

America was an unusual yacht, unlike any seen in England at that time. Not only was her hull shape and rig a departure from British custom, but her sails—made of cotton—were flatter and more efficient than the English hemp. (It is interesting to note that many of the recent America's Cup defenders have been superior at least partly because they set better sails than the challengers.) *America*'s hull was of a finer model, with her maximum beam and displacement well aft—a feature we recognize in more sophisticated times as being decidedly advantageous. She was also larger than most of her rivals— which also was to her advantage. All these pluses spelled a superior yacht, and today it is not surprising that the yachts in vogue in England at that time couldn't sail in the same water with her.

America was finally invited to sail with the Royal Yacht Squadron fleet in a race around the Isle of Wight on August 22, 1851. The prize for this race was the "Royal Yacht Squadron's Hundred Guineas Cup" and *America* won it easily. The press made a big thing of this event, *America*'s prowess, and the British lack of guts to accept her owners' challenge. A match was finally arranged—which *America* won. She was sold in England at the end of the yachting season, the whole adventure netting her owners $1,700—according to Boswell.†

It is important to remember the reception *America*'s owners received when assessing the early history of the America's Cup matches. In 1857, the surviving partners in the *America* syndicate

* Charles Boswell, *The America* (New York: David McKay, 1967, p. 42).
† Boswell, *The America*, p. 84.

presented to the New York Yacht Club the cup she had won from the Royal Yacht Squadron fleet. It was to be a perpetual challenge trophy to be challenged for in similar fashion to *America*'s original challenge to the British. Thus, when James Ashbury became the first America's Cup challenger in 1870, it is not surprising that he was required to sail his yacht to America on her own bottom, as *America* had, to race against the entire New York Yacht Club squadron, as *America* had raced against the entire Royal Yacht Squadron fleet, nor that his yacht, *Cambria*, was beaten.

Events evolve slowly from ideas. Ashbury suggested that he didn't have much of a chance racing against the whole fleet, so the conditions were changed for his rematch in 1871 with *Livonia*. This time the New York Yacht Club agreed to meet his challenger with a single yacht, but it reserved the right to choose the defender just before the race. Ashbury lost again.

The match became a true match with the first Canadian challenge in 1876 when the New York Yacht Club agreed to meet the challenger with a single defender. Now things were getting a bit fairer, but the result was the same.

And the result has been the same for 123 years since the *America* won her cup racing round the Isle of Wight. The matches have evolved into a very different event from that visualized by the donors of the Cup. The rules have been liberalized continually throughout the long history of the event, changed first by a new deed of gift from the sole surviving member of the syndicate in 1887 and again following World War II by court order to allow competition in smaller yachts. Still, the defender has always won—and only twice was the eventual outcome in serious doubt. It does not seem just to criticize the New York Yacht Club for alleged unfairness to a challenger when they have bowed to others' contentions that the game was one-sided and changed its character accordingly. Each challenger knew the rules before he came. Each challenger was beaten by a superior yacht and crew, not—as some have contended—because the New York Yacht Club changed the rules to suit itself.

Had Red Smith been aware of the early history of the America's Cup he doubtless would not have written that John Cox Stevens would have "saved us a century of strife" had he left the Royal Yacht Squadron Hundred Guinea Cup at the race track instead of the yacht club.

Had he done so the world would not have this interesting event, which stands unequaled as the longest record of domination in all of sports.

To many millions of fans—whether knowledgeable or ignorant of the sport—the America's Cup is the singular most shining example of national supremacy. No wonder that thousands flock to Newport, Rhode Island, every three or four years—whenever a match is run— just to be there and to be part of the spectacle.

That's why I was there—broken down on the finish line—and have been to every America's Cup either vicariously or in person since I was a kid, and that's why you and I have come together in these pages to explore the America's Cup challenge of 1974.

THE CHALLENGE

When *Intrepid* successfully defended the America's Cup in 1970 it
was generally conceded that she was at least no faster, and perhaps
a bit slower, than the Australian challenger *Gretel II*. The Aussies had
won a race and finished first in another only to be disqualified for a
foul at the start. The series was a close one, and it was won by the
New York Yacht Club defender probably because of exceptional preparedness and thoroughness. This is often characteristic of an
America's Cup defender who has won her berth through a hard-fought
summer-long racing campaign, while challengers often have had only
themselves or a "trial horse" with which to work into fighting trim.

    Because of the closeness of the series and the added interest of a
runoff between challengers, seen for the first time in 1970, it was
not surprising that several challenges, challengers perhaps sensing

2

that the hitherto impossible might soon be achieved, were received by
the New York Yacht Club following its successful defense. In order to
avoid frantic rushes to be first challenger, the Club has held to the
policy that challenges received within thirty days (now sixty days)
following a successful defense will be considered as having been
received simultaneously. Before the thirty days had passed, challenges
had been received from the Royal Thames Yacht Club in England, the
Royal Sydney Yacht Squadron and the Royal Perth Yacht Club in
Australia, and the Cercle de la Voilà de Paris and the Yacht Club
Hyers in France—five separate challengers.

Threatening to outdo France's Baron Marcel Bich in flamboyance
was Alan Bond, an uneducated, self-made millionaire real estate
developer from Perth, Western Australia. The America's Cup has
always hidden from commercialism behind a facade of purity—
sport for sport's sake. The New York Yacht Club has always refrained
from any sort of commercial ties involving the competition. To Alan
Bond, this was a lot of bull. Bond stated boldly and flatly at the outset
that his challenge was a commercial venture to advertise his desert-
by-the-sea development, Yanchep Sun City, and to promote Western
Australia to his ultimate benefit.

People were both shocked and annoyed by Bond's brash statements. Many Australians who knew of him were openly hostile and
critical. "Bond will ruin the America's Cup" and "You'll be sorry you
ever heard of him" were typical of the harsh statements coming from
Australian yachtsmen. Bond was also blatantly unsportsmanlike. He
used to his advantage the popular belief that the New York Yacht Club
had acted unfairly and in its own self-serving interest in the disqualification of *Gretel II* in the second race of the 1970 series. He
boasted that if he were confronted with similar "tactics" he would
resort to the courts in order to gain the Cup. He would not let the
"Yanks" push *him* around. Bond was obviously the sort of person who
would play upon any and all prejudices, including past allegations of
one-sided rulings, anything that he could dig up to intimidate the New
York Yacht Club and turn to his own advantage.

Such comments caused considerable concern among the conservative leaders of the Club. Although traditionally it is quite scrupu-
lous in conducting its private deliberations in private, one can easily
surmise that Bond's bad-mouthing hastened the club's decision—

which had already been agreed upon after the criticism caused by the
Gretel II protest—to have protests decided by an International Jury.*
In retrospect, it can be wondered why such action wasn't taken long
before, but only six America's Cup matches have been held since the
contest was revived in 12-Meters in 1958. With only one previous protest in history, and that in 1895, it is not so surprising that no problem was anticipated. With the *Gretel II–Intrepid* protest in 1970, it
became painfully clear that even under the best of circumstances and
the most clear-cut decisions, the New York Yacht Club was open to
criticism in deciding against a challenger. Thus it decided to turn
this power over to an International Jury, and Bond's appearance as a
challenger with a chip on his shoulder surely reinforced this decision.

Not only was Bond blatantly commercial and pugnacious, but he
was also cocksure that he would win. All it would take was enough
money and determination, he said, and he had plenty of both. No
expense would be spared to develop the fastest 12-Meter and the best
crew that the America's Cup contest had ever seen.

Bond bought *Gretel II* and successfully stifled the Sydney yachtsmen's challenge effort. With *Gretel* he felt he had an ideal point of
departure for Bob Miller to design a new and faster Twelve. Wasn't
Gretel acknowledged to be the world's fastest 12-Meter and weren't
the Australians proven in many competitions to be the world's best
sailors? Of course Bond would win the America's Cup. It was as good
as won as soon as he put his mind to winning it. A mounting place
was made for it in the Royal Perth Yacht Club (past challengers had
taken the precaution of making a box to ship the Cup home in, but no
one had ever been so confident as to make room for it in the clubhouse) and Yanchep Sun City was advertised in Australia as the site
of the 1977 America's Cup match.

Most people don't mind a certain amount of braggadocio on the
part of sport's figures—Muhammad Ali has made a career of it—but
Bond's habit of kicking and screaming in advance of imagined injus-

---

* An "international jury" is defined under International Yacht Racing Union
(IYRU) rule 77.5. The jury is chosen by the "organizing authority" (the New
York Yacht Club in this case), subject to the approval of the IYRU, "from
amongst yachtsmen who have an intimate knowledge and experience of the
racing rules."

tices was considered obnoxious by many, and it was to continue from
the time his challenge was first issued until well into the final series—
a span of nearly four years!

For a time in late 1970 and into 1971, it appeared that all the
challenges might founder. The New York Yacht Club asked the challengers to get together and decide how to conduct an elimination
series among five contenders. The clubs involved could not agree. In a
last attempt to save the series, the New York Yacht Club accepted the
single challenge of the Royal Thames Yacht Club and asked it to work
out an agreement among the interested parties that would allow the
selection of a single challenger.

The complexity of the problem was soon reduced by the reduc-
tion of the French and Australian challengers to one each. The field
was down to a more manageable number. Eventually, the Royal
Thames challenger failed to materialize, leaving that club with the
expense and responsibility for conducting an elimination series off
Newport without having any stake in the outcome. It was an excellent
situation for everyone except the Royal Thames treasurer.

Whereas Baron Marcel Bich had been visible and outspoken in
the 1970 challenge series—although in retrospect his antics seem
pale in comparison to Bond's—he was invisible or docile in this one.
He had ended his public appearances in 1970 with the proclamation
that he would never return to Newport. It was soon apparent, however, that the Baron still had "America's Cup fever" and that he was
continuing his efforts to win the Cup.

Bich recruited the Danish superstar Paul Elvström to skipper the
new French 12-Meter, which was to be designed by André Mauric, as
was the 1970 challenger, *France*. The Baron's spokesman-son, Bruno
Bich, who lives and works in New York, assured the curious world
that the headstrong Baron and the equally headstrong Elvström would
get along together. Elvström would have complete authority to run the
show. Could the French accept dictation from a Dane? Wouldn't this
make it more a Danish challenge than a French challenge? How could
such an arrangement work?

To the first question, Bruno answered that the French were being
realistic. Elvström offered them the best chance to win the America's
Cup, and that is what the Baron wanted to do. If he had to have a
Danish helmsman to win, he would have one. In answer to the second

question, Bruno said that the yacht would be designed and built in France, as the Cup conditions required, the crew would be French, and it would therefore be a French challenge, albeit with a Dane as helmsman.

It seemed an ideal marriage. The America's Cup was one of the only sailing challenges never attempted by Elvström. He wanted to do it, but surely he would never be able to put together a Danish challenge. Nowhere in France, perhaps nowhere in the world, was there Elvström's equal. If the Baron and "The King" (as yachtsmen everywhere call Elvström) could get along, it would be a serious and difficult challenge to defend against.

The sailing world was fascinated by the prospect of Paul Elvström—master of centerboarders, keelboats, and Half-Tonners—winner of more Olympic Gold Medals than any other sailor in history, meeting the "stuffy old men" of the New York Yacht Club. Elvström was the odds-on favorite to knock Bond off his high horse and give the defender a run the likes of which it had never seen before. The only question was whether Elvström could hold his temperamental nature in check and not blow the big challenge as he had blown the recent Olympics.

Whoever survived the battle between the French and the Australians would surely be a potent threat. Here, at last, was the type of intense racing series to rival those usually staged by the defending syndicates that made them hitherto invincible. If ever there was the potential for a challenger to win the America's Cup, this was it.

Alas, there were too many "ifs" in the French challenge, and too many of the ifs sprouted into debilitating problems.

Elvström took the French Twelves *Constellation* (the 1964 defender purchased by the Baron in 1967) and *France* to Denmark for modification and practical experience. *France* sank under tow in rough seas, because, said the French, the Danes had failed to station anyone aboard. She was recovered, but a large amount of French confidence in Elvström sank with her, and that was not recovered.

Elvström wormed his way into the design of the new French Twelve, and while the inner sanctum of a 12-Meter syndicate is closed to public view, it was apparent from a few unelaborated outbursts that French designer André Mauric was not happy with the decisions coming from Denmark. As the French challenge developed it looked more

Alan Bond. ". . . kicking and screaming in advance of imagined injustices . . ."

Bruno Bich. ". . . a man of his word."

and more like a Danish challenge sponsored by the Baron. Danes replaced Frenchmen in the crew, Elvström insisted on having more and more to say about the design, and, being a sailmaker, the sails were his as well. As building time neared it was obvious that the new Twelve was badly behind schedule. The Danish design team had been dragging its feet with indecision. Finally, in the early fall of 1973, Bruno Bich announced that the new boat would not be built. Elvström was fired. The challenge would still take place but with a revamped *France* and an entirely French effort.

Many doubted that the Baron would bother to try with an old wooden 12-Meter, but Bruno assured the world that they were quite serious. *France* would be much improved and would be a serious contender. He intimated that even if they lost they would gain valuable experience for the *next* challenge, but that they surely would be in Newport in 1974. The world was to learn that Bruno Bich was a man of his word.

France arrived in Newport in late July with an entirely French crew (except for Englishman Robin Fuger) headed by Jean-Marie Le Guillou, one of France's top helmsmen. Few observers took their challenge seriously—indeed the French seemed too relaxed to be serious—but they were there as promised.

While the French were screwing their single yacht together, two Australian crews were having at each other in Newport aboard *Gretel II* and *Southern Cross*.

Advance PR for *Southern Cross* had it that she was superfast off the wind, on the reaches and runs, and just as fast as *Gretel II* upwind. When they came together in Newport, it was clear that *Gretel II* was a bit faster upwind than *Cross*.

John Cuneo, who had been named by Bond as skipper, and Jim Hardy, who was *G II*'s skipper in 1970, swapped boats back and forth in a series of races in which Hardy was ultimately named to skipper *Southern Cross* in the challenge series against *France*.

After this announcement, Hardy sailed *Southern Cross* exclusively and gradually whipped her into shape so that she was consistently beating *Gretel II* upwind as well as down.

Ominously, Hardy was quoted by Bruce Kirby, writing in *Yacht Racing*, as saying that it was almost as if they were proving *Southern Cross* faster by slowing down *Gretel II*—failing to provide new sails for her and even failing to scrub her bottom!

Nevertheless, there was little doubt in anyone's mind that *Southern Cross* would beat *France* in their elimination series and would pose a serious threat to the defender. *Cross* was no dud—of that everyone was certain!

THE DEFENSE

Ted Turner had wanted to skipper a Twelve in the America's Cup ever since 1969 when he purchased the converted 12-Meter *American Eagle*, an unsuccessful defense candidate in 1964 and 1967. Turner, still very young for all his sailing experience, had been unable to find sufficient interest among his friends to put anything together in 1970, but he continued working toward a skipper's berth for 1974 and succeeded in joining the *Mariner* Syndicate. Turner's background made him a natural choice. In addition to being eager for the job, he probably had more 12-Meter experience than anyone else in the world, having sailed *Eagle* tens of thousands of miles in ocean races in the United States, in England, and in Australia. Granted, this experience was not the same that would be needed for match racing in the America's Cup, but Turner had plenty of class racing in both keelboats and centerboarders. He had several national and interna-

3

tional class titles to his credit and probably had more sailing trophies in his closets than anyone—surely more than anyone only thirty-six.

Turner had a difficult time breaking into the New York Yacht Club "establishment." He was a brash young man, bold in his social activities as well as on the race course, and some of his antics were not appreciated. He was kept out of the club the first time he was put up, but "old age" mellowed Turner a bit. He was elected to membership in 1973.

George Hinman, manager of the *Mariner* Syndicate, was quick to appreciate Turner's record and ability as a skipper. While Hinman was firmly entrenched in the New York Yacht Club—he was a former commodore and member of the America's Cup Committee—he was not the sort of person to let appearances and superficial behavior color his judgment of people's abilities. Turner and Hinman got along well, respected each other, and quickly developed a good working rapport.

The other key team members fitted together well too. Britton Chance had designed 5.5-Meters for Turner and also had a good record as a 12-Meter designer, having designed the 1970 French trial horse *Chancegger* and redesigned the successful 1970 defender *Intrepid*. Both Chance and Turner had also worked with builder Bob Derecktor in the past. Derecktor's experience as a builder and sailor was extensive. He'd built more aluminum yachts than any other builder in the United States. (All the new yachts were to be built in aluminum, now allowed owing to a rule change.) Derecktor was also to sail aboard the new Twelve. He had crewed in two previous America's Cup contenders.

It was a good team, highly regarded, with excellent talent from varied backgrounds. Chance surely would produce an interesting and innovative design, Derecktor would build it well, Turner could be expected to sail it well, and Hinman was capable of keeping the whole team functioning as a coordinated unit. In addition, Hinman would sail the trial horse *Valiant*, the unsuccessful Sparkman & Stephens design built by Derecktor in 1970, pushing the "first team" to excel as he had done as trial-horse contender in 1967 (*American Eagle*) and 1970 (*Weatherly*).

Before they had even begun, the *Mariner* Syndicate was halfway toward winning the America's Cup.

Were it not for the *Courageous* Syndicate, it would have been nearly a foregone conclusion that the *Mariner* group would defend the Cup, but the *Courageous* group had an even more solid background.

The basic *Courageous* Syndicate was headed by the same three men who ran the successful defenders of 1967 and 1970. William Strawbridge, Briggs Dalzell, and Burr Bartram had commissioned Sparkman & Stephens to design *Intrepid* in 1967. With Emil "Bus" Mosbacher at her helm she was an unbeatable superboat. The same syndicate commissioned Chance to redesign *Intrepid* for the 1970 series. They recruited Californian William Ficker and again put together an imposing win in the trials and defended the Cup. For 1974 they had largely the same crew headed by Ficker: they had returned to the acknowledged master of 12-Meter design—Olin Stephens of Sparkman & Stephens; and lined up the Minneford Yacht Yard of City Island, New York, which had built (or rebuilt) the last three defenders and had built an aluminum One Ton class yacht on "spec" just to gain experience in the material.

This group had to have an edge over any other. It had everything going for it. However, late in the fall of 1973, just as construction on the new yacht was being started, it was announced that a combination of the energy shortage, increased costs, and a sick stock market were forcing Strawbridge to give up as syndicate head and (presumably) principal financial backer. At the same time, Ficker announced that he had unexpected business commitments that required he step down as skipper.

Things looked bad for the *Courageous* group, but in spite of Strawbridge's announcement, Minneford's kept working on the yacht in hopes that the New York Yacht Club would come up with someone to replace Strawbridge. It did.

Robert McCullough had a great stake in the America's Cup. He had skippered *Constellation* as *Intrepid*'s trial horse in 1967 and had headed the syndicate and skippered the unsuccessful *Valiant* effort in 1970. He firmly believed in the Cup's traditions and vehemently defended them. Although McCullough was a member of the *Mariner* Syndicate, he stepped into the managership of *Courageous* and put the pieces back together in order to provide strong competition between contenders, as a hedge against *Mariner* being a dud, and to assure that the newest Stephens' design was available to the defense. He did not invest personally, he says, but he was able to persuade enough of his fellow club members to invest to assure a complete and proper campaign. He also enlisted Robert Bavier, who defended the Cup in *Constellation* in 1964, to take Ficker's place at the helm.

All was not complete equanimity, however. Most of the 1970 *Intrepid* crew chose not to sail without Ficker, and Bavier and McCullough recruited a new crew from among their East Coast establishment contacts.

Weakened though it was by uncertainty and change, the *Courageous* Syndicate still had to rate an even chance against the *Mariner* group, which had remained steadfast through the uncertain fall and winter of 1973–74.

Meanwhile, a group of West Coast yachtsmen had purchased *Intrepid.* Their plan was to have Olin Stephens redesign Britton Chance's redesign to bring her up to date (some said to return her more nearly to her original lines). San Diego boatbuilder Gerry Driscoll had wanted a shot at defending the America's Cup ever since he had built *Columbia* in 1964. Driscoll was to skipper *Intrepid* and he felt that he could turn the wooden yacht, which had been twice a defender, into a competitive Twelve by 1974 standards and make her the first yacht in history to defend the Cup three times. Many people felt that Driscoll was swimming upstream trying to make a wooden yacht competitive against the new aluminum hulls, but Driscoll did his homework carefully and figured it could be done by lightening the structure and simplifying the mechanics of the yacht.

Intrepid had at least one advantage over the new yachts. She had a spar with a titanium top section. Subsequent to the 1970 series the International Yacht Racing Union outlawed "exotic" materials such as titanium. The new yachts could not have them, but since *Intrepid* had been built before the edict she was allowed to use her original spar. It was a small advantage, but successful America's Cup defenders are made up of many very small advantages. Nothing is too small to be overlooked.

Intrepid had another big advantage. Although Driscoll made extensive alterations (the yacht looked as if it had washed up on somebody's beach when it arrived in his yard in June 1973 and was to look even worse before he was through tearing her apart) he still could finish her and have the crew sailing well before the East Coast yachts were completed. This would give Driscoll a significant head start in crew training, tuning, and sail selection—all more important race-winning factors than who has the fastest hull.

    Intrepid's early advantages were more than theoretical. "*Intrepid* enjoys advantages that no one really expected she'd have," wrote her sail trimmer John Marshall after the early trials. "First of all, the aluminum myth has been dispelled. The aluminum 12-Meters came out a bit heavier in their hull weight than people thought they would,

Intrepid, first to get sailing, simple, light, and proven.

and *Intrepid* was so skillfully lightened by Gerry Driscoll from her previous wooden construction that *Intrepid* actually enjoys a slight advantage in hull weight against the aluminum boats. The second advantage is that Driscoll did extensive tank testing in the Lockheed tank in California, using a much larger model than the Stevens tank in Hoboken, New Jersey, can handle. The larger model testing helps to avoid errors in stern configuration and allowed refinements in keel shape which have proven successful. . . .

"Speed is obviously terribly important in match racing, but just as important is the ability to sail the boat near her full potential all the time. On *Intrepid* the decision was made to strive for an extremely clean, simple deck layout with the important controls close at hand even if it meant locating some of the winches and hardware higher in the hull than on *Courageous*. The result has been advantageous; sail adjustments are easier to make and we can keep our sail trim more nearly optimum more of the time. When conditions change (the wind goes from light to fresh, or vice versa) or we encounter bad slop from the spectator fleet, *Intrepid* gains."

There was another subtle factor playing with people's judgments

Mariner, her radical square stern would either be super fast or super slow. (*Dan Nerney photo*)

about the new breed of Twelves. Many experts felt that all the designers had gone too far in refining the 1970 designs. Stephens' *Valiant* was certainly a disappointment. She did not appear to go to windward as well as expected and she exhibited persistent steering difficulties. While *Intrepid* as redesigned by Chance had defeated the Australian challenger *Gretel II*, many of these same experts felt that *Gretel II* was the better yacht and that she had been beaten by a superior crew. *G II* had many similarities, these experts said, to the superboat *Intrepid* of 1967. Had Chance slowed *Intrepid* down, and had Stephens, enticed into following Chance's features, produced a yacht that was actually slower than 1967 *Intrepid*? No one will ever know for sure, but the West Coast *Intrepid* Syndicate was fairly certain that they could make her a superboat once again by letting Stephens undo some of Chance's redesign and add some new developments that were destined for the *Courageous* Syndicate yacht.

At mid-March, before any outsiders had had glimpses of the three yachts, the *Mariner* Syndicate was proclaiming that they had an unbeatable design. *Courageous*'s people were quietly confident. *Intrepid*'s backers were saying that they had a very good chance.

Courageous: looking a lot like *Gretel II* but with a slotted bustle. (David Rosenfeld photo courtesy *Yacht Racing*)

Most of the "experts" had written off *Intrepid* as hopeless and were on the fence between the *Mariner* and *Courageous* syndicates. Some sage observers gave an early edge to *Intrepid* because of her advance shakedown and training sessions, but virtually no one gave her a chance to do much past the Observation Trial races in July.

Time would tell.

DESTINY FULFILLED

Usually it is sometime in April that the wraps come off the new defenders. By this time the yachts are hard to hide as they take shape and launching day nears. Also, it would be too late to use any "secrets" that an enemy camp might discover. It is important that the "enemy," as far as the defending syndicates are concerned, is each other. The challenger, whether it be French or Australian, is only a nebulous threat way down the line in September when the potential defenders have finished a grueling summer of trial races that result in one of them being selected as defender. Each syndicate has shrouded itself in secrecy, and now each releases choice bits of information testing the wind much as a timid bather tests the ocean by dipping a big toe before plunging in.

4

The first to get going was *Intrepid*. She was sailing in San Diego before the aluminum plating was finished on the two new yachts.

However, few were paying much attention to *Intrepid.* How could an old wooden boat expect to compete against the aluminum creations of Stephens and Chance? She was beating her trial horses *Columbia* and *Newsboy* (ex-*Easterner*), both circa 1958, but not by much. Big deal! Whatever was happening with *Intrepid* was ignored back East.

Public and competitors first got peeks at *Mariner* in late March as press releases and photographs began to come from Syndicate press-relations manager Bob Hall. *Mariner* was to be the name of the *Mariner* Syndicate's yacht, and while no photos were released to show what she looked like underwater, it was hinted that she was radical and believed to be the fastest 12-Meter yet to be conceived.

When the configuration of her underbody was revealed it was quite clear that if *Mariner* did not prove to be the fastest Twelve ever, she certainly was the most radical. Never before had a truncated stern such as this been tried in Twelves. The rationale was that the yacht's model had been tank-tested both with the stern faired to a conventional ending and with it chopped off abruptly. The tank showed there was no difference, so the stern was chopped much as if two giant whacks—one vertically upward and one horizontally inward—had been taken with a knife. The effect was supposed to produce a yacht that was considerably larger than the 12-Meter measurement rule allowed but cut off to fit within the rule. The principle was not unheard of, but never had it been applied in such extremes. There were actually two chops, a large one completely underwater aft of and above the rudder and a smaller flat one in the counter at the static waterline.

Courageous—the name of the *Courageous* Syndicate yacht—was completely unremarkable. (Nor was her name a surprise.) Stephens had been much more conservative in her design than he had been with *Valiant,* and except for an apparent horizontal ridge aft, in her "bustle" area, she appeared to be quite conventional. There were, of course, many subtle features that distinguished *Courageous* from other Twelves, but these could not be readily identified without access to the yacht's plans—which, of course, are not available to outsiders. In her overall concept she appeared reminiscent of *Gretel II,* the 1970 challenger.

Incredibly, *Valiant,* which was the only yardstick available by which to compare the new yachts, was modified by Chance to have some of *Mariner*'s radical features. The reasons for this were obscure. *Valiant* may not have been the fastest Twelve of the 1970 batch, but her relative performance was known. At least one foreign observer thought the defenders were playing a very dangerous game by eliminating their only known quantity.

Courageous and *Mariner* worked out separately on Long Island Sound in late May and early June. *Courageous* looked good, but there was nothing with which to compare her. *Mariner* was making quite a bit of fuss dragging her square stern through the water. One observer said the turbulence made so much noise that he could hear it over the sound of his chase-boat's outboard engine. However, the rest of her wave form looked very good.

The two yachts met for the first time during the New York Yacht Club Annual Regatta on Long Island Sound on June 1 and 2. *Courageous* gave *Mariner* a thorough beating in both races. *Mariner* people said their mainsail was terrible—which was confirmed by observers —and that they weren't fully tuned up yet. Nevertheless, it was beginning to appear that the design breakthrough that *Mariner* was supposed to represent might have broken through in the wrong direction.

The first match racing took place in the Preliminary Trial Races beginning June 24 off Newport on the America's Cup Course. *Intrepid*'s early edge in tuning and crew training paid off, and she emerged with the most wins and a record of 5 and 2, being beaten by *Courageous* twice and beating her twice. *Mariner* was able to beat only her syndicate mate, *Valiant*. The latter beat no one.

While people were beginning to feel that *Mariner* was, perhaps, a colossal blunder it was not clear that she was not competitive until she actually met *Courageous* and *Intrepid* in the trials. In an outstanding and unusual segment on a CBS television program on the series filmed by Jim Lipscomb, Ted Turner and his tactician Dennis Conner are shown as they meet *Intrepid* for the first time. *Mariner* gets the start, but *Intrepid* quickly works up underneath, "pointing higher and footing faster," Conner tells Turner. Looks of disappointment and futility grow on the faces and in the voices of Turner and Conner. "This is faster than we've ever gone," says Turner in disbelief that *Intrepid* is faster still. *Mariner* is sailing faster than she is theoretically supposed to as they realize that nothing they can do will stop *Intrepid*. To a racing sailor this short segment of *cinéma vérité* must rate as one of the most poignant ever captured on film. For the *Mariner* crew it was the beginning of a long and bitter downhill slide to oblivion.

Mariner was a disaster. She and *Valiant* returned to Derecktor's to be rebuilt.

As will happen, any time things don't go well in a big project such as a 12-Meter campaign, the people involved start looking at each other and pointing fingers. Hinman blasted Chance, claiming that the extensive modifications to *Valiant* were made without his consent and against his wishes. He ordered *Valiant* restored as nearly as possible to her 1970 configuration. Chance blamed Turner for not getting the most out of *Mariner*, and there were several bitter exchanges between them, Chance saying that Turner was butchering the fastest 12-Meter ever built. Turner countered with an exchange that was to become legend before the summer was over and that went something like this: "Brit, do you know why there are no fish with square tails? Because all the pointed-tail fish caught them and ate them." It was reported that Turner walked away a few paces then turned and said to Chance, "Even shit's pointed at both ends!"

Chance was reported to have an alternate stern design ready in the eventuality that the chopped-off one didn't work. However, while the old stern was sawed off, work did not begin immediately on the new one.

I was visiting with Bob Hall in Newport one day in mid-July and asked him why the delay. "They went back to the tank (Stevens Institute Davidson Laboratory testing tank) and found a significant improvement over the modification that was originally planned," said Hall. Rather sarcastically I asked him how they could tell that "significant improvement" from the one that suggested the original disastrous configuration. Bob's reply was, under the circumstances, very appropriate: "Don't ask me, I just put out what they tell me to."

Back in Newport, *Courageous* and *Intrepid* were undergoing modifications of their own, which were much less drastic than *Mariner*'s and *Valiant*'s. *Intrepid*'s rudder was moved aft several inches to improve her balance and control, and *Courageous* had some of her ballast removed (which would allow a bit more sail area) to improve her light wind performance.

When the bell rang for the second round—the Observation Trials —*Courageous, Intrepid,* and *Valiant* answered. *Mariner* was still in

Mamaroneck getting her new "breakthrough" stern welded on. Observers peeking inside Derecktor's shed said the new stern looked very much like the one on *Courageous*.

The big question: Could *Mariner* overcome the disadvantage of a late start—even if her modifications did make her competitive—and become a contender in the Final Trials? It was doubtful, but it was shaping up as a summer of surprises. Anything was possible.

Intrepid and *Courageous* both designed by Olin Stephens and both very close in speed.

NEWPORT

5

Exquisite attention to detail of the Newport Restoration Foundation is exemplified by this house on Pelham Street.

I am told by proud Newport residents that their city was once the largest among the American Colonies. It is hard to imagine today, because Newport—at least that charming part of it around the harbor —is small enough that an automobile is a liability instead of a necessity. Certainly, Newport is little bigger now than it was in Colonial days.

Newport has always had a distinctive charm, although today it is quite different from what it was when I first saw it about twenty-five years ago. I'm not sure whether the overall effect is an improvement —perhaps we could call it a draw. Today Newport is charming in many ways. It has lost something of its past, but the net effect is of a town that one can enjoy immensely and in great variety.

For as long as I've known Newport, it has been a "Navy town." My first memories of it contain 40-foot liberty launches shuttling back and forth between what is now the site of the Treadway Inn and Goat Island. I remember particularly the coxswain in the sternsheets with his tiller and bell, ringing up full reverse when he practically could have reached the engine controls himself and surely could have whispered to the "engineer" to put the damn thing in reverse. But that would not have been the "Navy" way.

The Navy is gone now along with its liberty launches, coxswains, Shore Patrol, and carousing sailors staggering from bar to bar along Thames Street (pronounced as it's spelled, to the utter amazement of the English). In fact, much of Thames Street is gone now, and this is part of the loss of modern Newport. While the buildings that have been removed to make way for "America's Cup Avenue" were decrepit and the bars they housed mostly degenerate dives, they were an inseparable part of the Newport of old as was the cobblestone narrow Thames Street itself and its endless stream of cars crawling in slow motion. The Cameo Bar, which the Aussies adopted and christened the "Royal Cameo Yacht Squadron" in 1962; the Roman Gardens, where you could get an inexpensive glass of beer and an excellent pizza; the Tides Inn, where you thought breakfast was going to give you food poisoning but it never did—these landmarks are gone forever to make way for modern Newport and broad America's Cup Avenue. Some—not all—would say good riddance.

Fortunately, the Newport Restoration Foundation made possible by the liberal spending of Doris Duke, the Carolina Piedmont region Duke power heiress, is saving the truly good buildings in Newport. Institutions like The Candy Store were moved out of range of the wrecking balls. Mario's Deli and the Army/Navy Surplus Store found new quarters. The genuine Colonial-period buildings have been or are being renovated, and enough of Thames Street remains narrow and cobbled to preserve its heritage.

Unfortunately, the reconstruction around America's Cup Avenue was not quite finished for the summer of 1974 although it had been promised that it would be. Those things happen, and once one got used to the way things were, it was hardly noticed. The cars still crept down Thames Street slower than the pedestrians, The Candy Store is better than ever both inside and out, Bowen's Wharf is an incredibly apt and practical restoration, and one can still get a towel, soap, and a shower at the Seaman's Institute for only a quarter—if you're a man, that is (some things never change!).

above. Advertising agencies and publicity agents had a field day in Newport attempting to get some ruboff of the glamour that surrounds an America's Cup series. Here a director poses a topless model for a photographer (hidden behind rocks) and unwittingly for another photographer passing by aboard *Gamecock*. The flare from the author's lens sent them scurrying for cover.

below. The Elms mansion with its statuary, terraced gardens, and vast expanse of lawn. Once a mere summer home, it is now a tourist curiosity and the site of the New York Yacht Club's welcoming cocktail party the night before the America's Cup series begins.

above left. Picturesque signs hang above the shops along Thames Street.

above right. Buildings along the cobblestoned waterfront at Bowen's Wharf, a classic restoration.

right. An impromptu gallery in a shed on Commercial Wharf displays paintings and old America's Cup memorabilia.

The Twelves were not the only spectacular sailing vessels to be seen in Newport. Here the schooner *Bill of Rights* enters the harbor accompanied by a replica of a nineteenth-century whaleboat.

The Navy has been going from Newport for years. The last vestiges of its buildings on Goat Island have disappeared and there is now a bridge, condominium apartments, marina, and large modern Sheraton Hotel there. While the Goat Island station has been shut for quite a while, there were still a large number of Navy personnel stationed up the Bay until 1973, when the last base was finally closed. All that remains is the Naval War College.

The Navy's departure has had a considerable economic effect on Newport and all of the Narragansett Bay area (Quonset Naval Air Station on the west side of the Bay is closed too). There is great fear that Newport may not be able to make it without the Navy, and certainly those shopkeepers and apartment owners who relied on the Navy for business and tenants have had a rough time and may face rougher times with no America's Cup until 1977. Nevertheless, there is the feeling among many local businessmen that now that the Navy has finally gone, it will be a good thing. They will find out if they can make it on the tourist business—the only remaining industry—and if they can, they say it will be good in the long run. I even heard a shopkeeper express the *fear* that the Navy might have to come back if the Mediterranean Fleet was forced to leave Greece.

Newport has always been an adventure town—particularly in an America's Cup year. Whether one was racing down route 138 from New York trying to catch the last ferry, getting caught climbing in the window of The Black Pearl because that's where the action was and they wouldn't let anyone in the door, watching "Monsieur Le Baron" punching out a French cameraman, having a before-breakfast Bloody Mary passed through the porthole of a Chinese junk by the lithe arm of the owner's girl, getting caught in The Port O'Call woman's shower with someone else's wife, just walking down Thames Street looking in the shop windows or socializing in The Candy Store, Newport was always fun.

The ferry is gone, replaced by a bridge that costs two dollars one way. (If you know about such things, you buy one trip and nine tokens for ten dollars and sell eight tokens to the desk clerk at the Treadway Inn for a dollar each.) One no longer has to plan his arrival in Jamestown or wait in line for an hour and a half and three ferries. The Black Pearl is no longer the "in" place, so you wouldn't be caught dead climbing in the window. "Monsieur le Baron" is much more subdued than in 1970 and will be hard to find. The owner of the Chinese junk didn't bring his girl this time. The woman in the shower has gone back to her husband. But you can still do similarly outrageous things. You can still walk down Thames Street, be charmed by the beautifully restored sea-captains' homes, and look in the shop windows. And whether you're inside looking out or outside looking in, the view from The Candy Store is just great.

Newport is still fun, and in an America's Cup year it's *incroyable!*

Not all the yachts in Newport were "spit and polish."

PUTTING IT ON THE LINE
BY JEFF HAMMOND

A script unfolded in Newport in July that would have made any
Hollywood producer's eyeballs light up with dollar signs. All that was
lacking was a Fitzgerald to write a few extra lines. The weather was
in Technicolor for nearly the entire month with a powder-blue sky
and wisps of cloud for the backdrop. The stage was the deep, indigo-
blue water of Rhode Island Sound. Fresh, crisp air that made just
being alive and being there more important than whatever mortals
were doing in their racing machines swept over the boats, their men,
and Newport all month long. The docks, restaurants, sidewalk cafés,
and open verandas were filled with lithe, tanned Newport women
and their well-dressed, handsome escorts, reveling in the balmy

First published in *Yachting*, September, 1974, titled "The Script Changes at
Newport," by Jeff Hammond. Reprinted with permission.

breezes and talking of the July trials for the America's Cup. They had
much to talk about.

To this idyllic July America's Cup scenario was added a bold brush stroke right out of Hollywood that gave the month its high drama. *Intrepid*, the proud old wooden warhorse that had twice before defended the America's Cup, the boat that had been counted out of the action against the modern aluminum Twelves, the boat with topsides a patchwork of touch-up paint jobs and that was using a 1967 boom and old winches, the contender championed by a low-budget syndicate that was actually soliciting money among the yachting populace—*Intrepid*, the boat with so much going against her, slammed through the July trials in such a decisive fashion that it would have brought tears to the eyes of any Saturday matinee crowd.

Had only movie director Francis Ford Coppola been there! *Courageous*, the sleek new glistening white Twelve designed by S & S and built in four months by Minneford's yard at City Island, New York, with the tall, composed Bob Bavier at the helm, had been the early favorite because she had so much going for her. Yet in the July trials it was *Courageous* that was fraught with problems. From the beginning her sails were too full and her ultramodern Kevlar main was constantly in a state of recutting. From early summer, gear had been failing—first the jib halyard sheaves up the mast, then the stainless-steel dogbones that connected her starboard chainplates to the keel snapped in a fresh breeze, and finally, just four minutes before a start against *Intrepid*, the backstay crane at the masthead bent dangerously, threatening to topple the spar when one of the crew was slow in taking up on a running backstay after a jibe. The boat that had the edge on winning starts during the June trials began losing starts in July, and in the first few races was unaccountably late at the starting line. Most surprising of all, *Courageous* seemed to be only as fast as *Intrepid* in light air and a fraction slower in moderate wind strengths. In the evenings, the *Courageous* crew retired to the palatial Hammersmith Farms (which was rented to the syndicate for the summer by the Auchincloss family) and the crew discussed events of the day over cocktails and hors d'oeuvres on the mansion's patio. No one would have been surprised had Robert Redford and Mia Farrow walked in wearing their 1920s costumes to join the discussions and cast their eyes over the rolling green lawn that undulates down the hillside to the sparkling blue waters of Narragansett Bay. Indeed, at water's edge was the lonely and elegant white pier used in the filming of *The Great Gatsby*, with the film's blinking green light replaced by the syndicate's #26 pennant.

Yet the cast of characters and the July drama were still not complete. The trial-horse *Valiant*, sailed by former N.Y.Y.C. commodore George Hinman, gamely tried to keep up with the other Twelves but was plagued with so many mishaps that she became Newport's hard-luck boat. In one race the bottom half of her new rudder fell off and later *Intrepid* tacked so close aboard that her transom-mounted turning block gouged a deep hole in *Valiant* at the waterline. Later, when *Valiant* was being put back in the water after repairs, a cable on the traveling lift parted and *Valiant* dropped ten feet into the water, throwing one of her crew over the side in what could have been a tragic accident.

By the end of the July trials in Newport *Intrepid* had tallied a score of 5 wins and 2 defeats against *Courageous* and *Valiant*. Her racing record for both the June and July trials was 12 wins and 5

Courageous "home," Hammersmith Farm, being passed by Alan Bond's chartered yacht, *Captiva*.

losses, the most impressive of the four boats slugging it out for the favor of the N.Y.Y.C.'s selection committee. Most significant, *Intrepid* defeated the new *Courageous* in four out of six contests in July—two of which were held over a full-length America's Cup course.

Courageous ended up with a 7–4 score in July (11–6 for the combined trials) with *Valiant* posting 1–8 in July (1–12 for both trials).

"UP 'THE PEOPLE'"

Here is my dollar to help the Intrepid *win. I'm eight years old and I like to sail.*

> Good Luck,
> Greg Lochner
> Coos Bay, Oregon

7

For the first time in America's Cup history, a syndicate solicited funds from the general public to help defray the costs of the campaign. This was made possible by a favorable tax ruling, which allowed the Seattle Sailing Foundation to underwrite the campaign as a training exercise for young sailors. Donations to the *Intrepid-*West Syndicate through the Foundation are deductible from the donor's federal income tax. (*Mariner* also had this advantage through

donations to the U.S. Merchant Marine Academy. *Courageous* did not,
being entirely privately operated.)

The idea of an old wooden boat from the West Coast on a limited budget taking on the megabucks of the Eastern Establishment caught the imagination of ordinary people everywhere. *Intrepid* supporters conducted what they called a "nickle, dime, and dollar" fund-raising effort selling posters, buttons, and other *Intrepid* material. "Knock on Wood" bumper stickers, a reference to the supposed inferiority of *Intrepid*'s wooden hull to the newer aluminum designs, appeared everywhere. (These were countered by *Courageous* stickers reading "26 Pick Up Sticks," the "26" referring to *Courageous*'s sail number.)

The *Intrepid* Syndicate did nothing to dispel this image—in fact, they used it to help promote their cause. Speaking of their fund-raising effort, Business Manager Dick Friel said, "Because the *Intrepid* is 'the people's boat' and as long as we keep winning races, we are showing the public, which is supporting us, that they are a part of this year's America's Cup campaign."

That, perhaps, is the best point about this year's series. Because of *Intrepid* and because her backers went to the general public for support, the public could be involved in the America's Cup for the first time in its history. And they really got turned on.

Letters such as Greg Lochner's, but from adults and containing more than a dollar, poured into Friel's office. The money flowed in although it was not quite enough to meet their budget of $750,000, relative chickenfeed compared with the multimillion-dollar expenses reported by others. Even an English boatbuilder was caught up in the spirit, and after a day aboard *Intrepid*'s tender pledged the equivalent of a new genoa (about $2,500) to the syndicate . . . and for him it wasn't tax deductible!

One quickly caught the spirit that infected the *Intrepid* group. Whereas other syndicates had crew members to do the sailing and other "crew members" to do some of the menial labor, *Intrepid*'s crew were also her laborers. It was not uncommon to see Skipper Gerry Driscoll and Syndicate Manager Sunny Vynne under *Intrepid* rubbing down her bottom with the rest of the crew. Seeing John Marshall, prominent East Coast sailmaker, and Andrew McGowan, naval architect (and both successful skippers in their own right), one observer said, "Look at that, will you, John and Andy there under *Intrepid* with grinders and sanders getting *dirty* yet. I've never seen those guys work *that* hard before."

It was this sort of team*work* ashore as well as on the race course that helped weld *Intrepid* into a winning effort. It showed on the scoreboard, it showed to outside observers, and the people responded.

Shouts of "Go 'The People,' " "Hurray for the people's yacht," and "Up 'The People,' " would mingle with a simple "Go *Intrepid*" when she would do well on the race course or when she returned to the dock after a successful day.

People would line the pier at Williams and Manchester Shipyard, where *Intrepid*'s hoist was, and the dock opposite *Intrepid* at Mack's Clam Shack, to cheer her when she came in. Some would wait for hours, not knowing if the trial races were long or short, if they had been delayed, or if the Committee had decided on a second race for that day. Every evening there would be over a hundred spectators on hand to cheer *Intrepid*'s arrival. If she had won that day their jubilation would know no bounds.

One evening when *Intrepid* had lost two races to *Courageous*, both on bad breaks, the *Intrepid* crew was particularly subdued when

left. Andy McGowan was hoisted aloft after almost every race to clear the head of *Intrepid*'s mainsail.

right. *Intrepid* in her special "drying-out" hoist, on which she was lifted after each race.

Racing for the America's Cup, 1974

they got to the dock. The applause was there but brief and polite. During a lull in the general hubbub, a voice boomed out over the crowd. "That's okay, *Intrepid*, you'll show 'em tomorrow!" The crowd broke into a rousing cheer, and the long faces on *Intrepid*'s dock turned to appreciative grins. In fact, they did "show 'em tomorrow" . . . and tomorrow and tomorrow, as *Intrepid* beat *Courageous* three in a row.

About one-third of the crowd that waited for *Intrepid* each day applaud her arrival after a successful day.

The more she won, the more people came to the dock and the more people sent in money. Vynne and Friel were overwhelmed and ecstatic, as was everyone involved. The goodwill was so heavy in the air it threatened the fog for palpability.

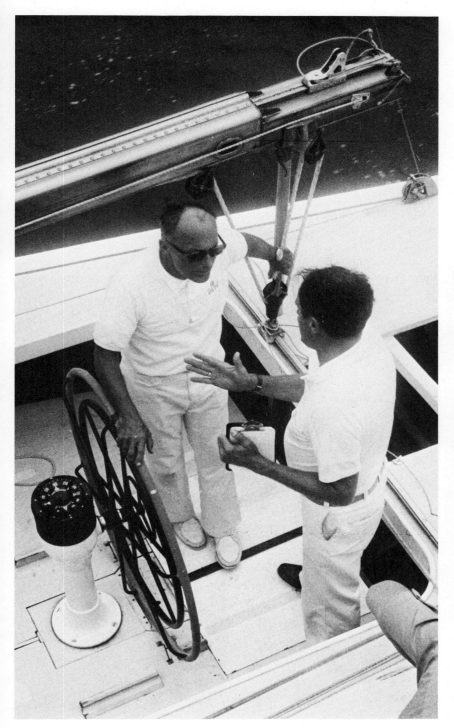

left. As soon as *Intrepid* was alongside her tender, Syndicate Manager
Sunny Vynne was aboard to discuss
the day's race with skipper
Gerry Driscoll.

right. Going over notes of obser-
vations from *Intrepid*'s tender.

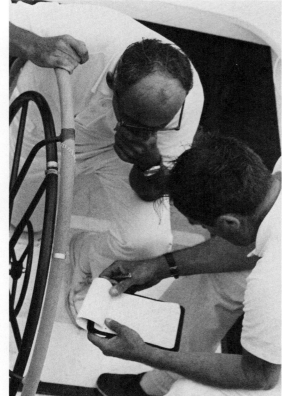

above.   1958's defending skipper,
Briggs Cunningham, now a fellow
Californian, listens to Gerry Driscoll
describe how *Intrepid* beat
Courageous.

below.   "Come on, Baby, dig in
there Girl. . . ." Mrs. Driscoll cheers
her husband's victory . . .

. . . and Gerry waves back clutching an after-race soda. Bill Buchan looks puzzled, probably trying to figure out how he's going to steer *Intrepid* back to Newport, unwrap and eat the sandwich in his left hand, and drink the Coke perched on the deck.

AUGUST—LOG OF THE "GAMECOCK"

The New York Yacht Club's final trials to select a defender began on August 15, and while they were racing on the America's Cup course 7½ miles south-southwest of Brenton Reef tower, the Australian-French series began August 22 nine miles to the southwest at the U.S. Navy torpedo buoy "A."

We went out each day in *Gamecock* to whichever race course we thought would provide the most excitement, and then transferred from one course to the other when things got dull where we were. Fortunately, there were few days of conflict. When the Aussies and French were staging their more interesting races, the New York Yacht Club was taking the day off. As a result we missed very little of significance on either course.

8

AUSTRALIA VERSUS FRANCE

Aboard Gamecock: *Thursday, August 22*
Weather: Hazy (clearing later). Wind ENE, shifting to SE 5–8 knots.

Southern Cross *slips out of the harbor without fanfare promptly at 0900.* France *leaves a few minutes later, and the spectator fleet straggles out to the torpedo range up to an hour later.* Courageous *and* Intrepid *have the day off—a break for the spectators. All the talk generated over the summer—the smoke screens designed to confuse the opposition and the public—is about to be blown away in the hard realities of yachts and crews coming together on the race course.*

Both yachts milled around each other briefly before the start. Australia's Jim Hardy won the controlling position, forcing *France*'s Jean-Marie Le Guillou to jibe for the line. *Southern Cross* tacked, thereby gaining important distance to windward, and the fate of the French yacht was sealed.

Still, at this point, it was uncertain if *France*, with clear air, would be fast enough to sail out from under *Southern Cross*. Her advance "PR" had billed her as best in light air. If she were faster, *France* could get away.

She didn't. Within a very few minutes *France* tacked to clear her wind, and the race was virtually over. *Southern Cross* led at each mark, extending her lead until, at the finish, she was over 7 minutes ahead.

The only question that remained throughout the day was whether the yachts would finish within the 5½-hour time limit. The wind faded in the middle of the race, but it picked up for the final beat to allow *Southern Cross* to finish with about half an hour to spare.

If the race wasn't particularly exciting, there was tragic excitement in another quarter. A helicopter piloted by John Wallace and carrying CBS cameraman Delos Hall and technician Robert Oddo crashed in the midst of the spectator fleet. Quick action by Andrew White from *Southern Cross*'s tender *Offsider* and from other spectators and Coast Guard personnel saved the lives of Wallace and Hall, who were removed from the overturned helicopter. However, Oddo apparently drowned before they could get him out.

The helicopter had been flying about 150 feet above the water. Suddenly there was a "pop" followed by a swishing sound. I turned just in time to see it splash inverted into the water about 500 yards from *Gamecock.*

Hall was taken to Newport by one of the fast New York Yacht Club tenders while a Coast Guard Cutter (CG 41321) took Wallace and Oddo to Point Judith. Wallace and Hall were seriously injured, but both recovered.

Aboard Gamecock: *Friday, August 23*
Weather: Hazy followed by some sun and rain. Weak cold front approaching and passing about 1600. Wind light and variable.

France *and* Southern Cross *meet for the second time today while* Courageous *and* Intrepid *resume their labors, following their day off to watch the first race of the challengers' series. Unless Jean-Marie Le Guillou is more aggressive at the start and can put* France *in control early, it is feared that she will have little chance of beating* Southern Cross.

Southern Cross starts with a safe leeward position on *France . . .*

At the start of the second race between *France* and *Southern Cross,* Jim Hardy appeared to have a controlling position on Jean-Marie Le Guillou, but then broke off, letting the French yacht go. Both

yachts started with clear air, but *France* was slightly ahead and to leeward. She appeared to be in the better position.

Southern Cross gradually worked out to windward and ahead, forcing *France* to tack. An approaching thunderstorm temporarily killed the wind and lifted both yachts to the lay line of the weather mark. However, the wind soon filled in again from more or less the same direction and gave neither yacht a discernible advantage. When they eventually crossed, *Southern Cross*, on starboard, did so ahead of *France*, but the yachts were too close for the Australians to cover. For some inexplicable reason *France* tacked! Not only was she headed in the same direction as *Southern Cross*, but she was heading away from the approaching storm, which ought to have favored the yacht closest to it. Once again, *Southern Cross* tacked and crossed *France*— this time more easily. *France* then split tacks, but that was it. The final margin was 3 minutes, 37 seconds. It was a close race but the outcome was never in doubt.

Jim Hardy said later that he thought *France* had sailed faster than *Southern Cross* at times. The general feeling was that both

... leads narrowly at the first mark ...

yachts were very close in speed potential, but that the French were making relatively many small mistakes that were costing them important advantages and missed opportunities. With more aggressive starting tactics to put them in control of the Aussies, the French crew could win. However, betting was that they wouldn't even win one race.

Aboard Gamecock: *Saturday, August 24*
Weather: Hazy, followed by dense fog from about 1400 to 1500.
Wind SW 12–15 knots.

This is the day the French say they need to do better. According to Bruno Bich, the wind is just right.

. . . and *France* rounds in pursuit, setting her spinnaker for the reaching leg.

Both yachts were aggressive at the start with circling beginning at the 10-minute gun. Jean-Marie Le Guillou had excellent control

over the Aussies, but he appeared to let *Southern Cross* get away. This seemed strange when it was most likely that the only way the French yacht could win would be to get in a commanding position at the start and hold a close cover thereafter. After 10 minutes with both yachts sailing in clear air, *France* tacked onto starboard and failed to cross *Southern Cross*. It appeared that the third race would go to the Australians like the previous two—close but decisive.

But the fog intervened. Visibility went to a few hundred feet while the yachts were on the first reach. *Southern Cross* blew her spinnaker and lost a bit of her lead while it was replaced. (Her navigator estimated they lost .4 knots for a minute and fifty seconds.) The Aussies said that because of the fog they held high of the reaching mark and did not see it. They estimated that they left a 400-yard margin, but admitted that it wasn't sighted—nor were they reported by the stake boat as having rounded. *France* apparently found the mark and caught up—coming together with *Southern Cross* on the second reach. Both yachts were "dead even" by both crews' accounts when the Royal Thames Race Committee ordered the race abandoned.

It was a morale-boosting day for *France*, but moral victories don't go in the record book.

Aboard Gamecock: *Sunday, August 25*
Weather: Clear with thin haze. Wind ENE 4–5 knots.

France *puts* Southern Cross *away just before the start, forcing the Australian yacht above the line before the gun. However, the French skipper then allows the Aussies to get back, and* Southern Cross *wins another start.*

---

opposite. Jean Marie Le Guillou forces his Aussie rival above the line . . .

. . . but then lets him come back just before the start.

The wind shifted but remained light. The shift favored *Southern Cross*, and she took a commanding lead. Continuing wind shifts played havoc with the race course and the competitors. *France* nearly caught up to *Southern Cross* on two occasions—closing the gap to within 16 seconds at the first mark. However, the wind remained light as well as variable throughout the day, and the yachts failed to finish within the 5½-hour time limit. No race.

Both yachts start even with
Southern Cross in the controlling
position to windward.

Aboard Gamecock: *Monday, August 26*
Weather: Clear with haze. Wind SE 10–14 knots.

For the first time in the series, France gets the start on Southern
Cross. *It is a narrow margin and both yachts have clear air.
Jean-Marie Le Guillou appears to be more aggressive in his starting
tactics, but it may be that Jim Hardy is playing his starts more
conservatively, knowing that his yacht is faster than* France.

France's lead was short-lived. *Southern Cross* sailed away from
the French yacht soon after the start and continued to extend her
margin in the relatively steady moderate winds. At the finish *France*
was a dismal 6 minutes, 59 seconds behind—nearly a mile in distance!

Southern Cross takes the final gun with *France* far astern.

France signals that she does not wish to race tomorrow. No doubt they are hoping for a major miracle. Nothing less will help.

Aboard Gamecock: *Wednesday, August 28*
Weather: Overcast with limited visibility. Wind SW at 10–12 knots.

With no change in the weather pattern, today surely will be France's last day. It seems hardly possible that she can do anything significant against the Australian yacht.

Once again Jean-Marie Le Guillou won the start from Jim Hardy, but the appearance of more aggressive starting tactics by the French helmsman must be tempered with the now-certain knowledge that *Southern Cross* could easily outsail *France* under these conditions; Hardy didn't *need* to win the start.

Southern Cross took the lead about 10 minutes after the start, and the outcome was never in doubt thereafter. The margin at the finish was 4 minutes, 22 seconds, not as decisive as the previous race, but a sound thrashing nonetheless.

Bruno Bich admitted after this final race that he thought *France* was slower than *Southern Cross*. However, he felt that his yacht was considerably improved over 1970. In his statement to the press Bich said, "Jean-Marie, myself, and the whole crew obviously feel disappointed in having lost four to nothing. However, we don't regret in any way to have come here. We have learned a lot and we are now prepared to help *Southern Cross* to win the America's Cup."

Bich was asked if his father would challenge again.

"The final decision about a future challenge by our syndicate will be made after the series between the Americans and *Southern Cross*," Bich said. "However, we came here with the intention to challenge again and right now this intention still stands. But the final decision will be made after the finals."

To the same question, Alan Bond replied, "I think the question will be, 'Will America challenge the Australian's Cup in 1977?'"

Asked what he thought *Southern Cross*'s chances were against either *Courageous* or *Intrepid*, Bruno Bich answered, ". . . I think that they are the best prepared challengers that I have seen and that they do have a *real* chance for the Cup. . . ."

Baron Bich, in his white yachting dress, played "low profile" all summer, watches *France* bow to the Aussies from aboard his three-masted schooner *Shenandoah*.

THINNING THE FIELD

"We have done so much with so little for so long that we could go on doing something with nothing forever."
Jeff Neuberth, Valiant *crew member*

9

Mariner returned to Newport with her new aft end just before the final trials were to begin. If she was to do anything, it would have to be immediately or surely the America's Cup Committee would eliminate her and her syndicate mate, *Valiant.* This would allow *Intrepid* and *Courageous*—now clearly established as the favorites— to have at it seriously every day.

In a desperate attempt to get something going, Ted Turner was replaced as skipper of *Mariner* by Dennis Conner, who had been *Mariner*'s tactician and then *Valiant*'s helmsman. Conner, a Congressional Cup champion from California, was eager for the job. He didn't go to Newport just to be tactician for someone else, he is reported to have said, and it is not difficult to imagine that he promoted himself at Turner's expense. His main strength over Turner was in his starting tactics. Perhaps if he could win the starts with *Mariner,* she could stay ahead. That was the plan and Turner and Conner switched mounts literally in midstream.

Mariner continued to be disappointing. She was beaten by *Intrepid* in the first race of the final trials, and the end appeared nearer still.

Aboard Gamecock: *Tuesday, August 20*
Weather: Clear. Wind 10 knots.

Conner has been able to do no better than Turner. He managed to beat Turner and Valiant *in the second race of the final trials, but with* Valiant *matched against* Intrepid *and* Mariner *against* Courageous *in the third race of the final trials, it looks like showdown day for the* Mariner Syndicate. *If she can beat* Courageous, Mariner *might be alive for another day. If she loses, surely the Committee will be paying her a visit and give their traditional, "Gentlemen, thank you very much," meaning the syndicate's services are no longer required.*

Neither *Mariner* nor *Valiant* were a match for their third race rival. *Intrepid* assumed the lead at the start and extended it at each mark until she was 9 minutes ahead of *Valiant* at the end of the second beat. *Courageous* had a similar lead on *Mariner.* In fact, *Courageous* was threatening to overtake *Valiant,* which had started ten minutes ahead. Both defeats were decisive and significant.

A few minutes after *Valiant* and *Mariner* docked at Newport Shipyard, the uniformed and distinguished-looking members of the New York Yacht Club America's Cup Committee, led by former Commodore Henry Morgan, came alongside to give George Hinman and his crews the bad news. There was no need for words to tell them that they had been eliminated; it was obvious. Neither *Mariner* nor *Valiant* was equal to the task of defending the America's Cup.

There were tears in his eyes when George Hinman, a former

commodore and America's Cup Committeeman himself, thanked the
Committee and his crews. "I suppose we have made a contribution in
our own way," said Hinman, but the implication was that the contribution was far short of expectations, if not downright obscure.

Ted Turner, as he watched the Committee's *Navette* head back to
Goat Island said, "Let's go some place and get a shooter." What else
was there to do?

Mariner's last effort, literally miles
behind *Courageous*, confirmed the
Committee's conviction that she was
not up to defending the Cup.

George Hinman, syndicate manager, thanks the crews of *Mariner* and *Valiant* for their efforts. After the America's Cup Committee members have come to give them the bad news . . .

. . . *Navette* takes them back to seclusion on Goat Island.

Aboard Gamecock: *Wednesday, August 21*
Weather: Clear but hazy. Wind ESE, light.

After a postponement to wait for breeze, the America's Cup Race Committee sends Intrepid *and* Courageous *off in very light east-southeast winds. Both yachts come together shortly after the 10-minute gun.* Courageous *seems to get on* Intrepid's *stern rather easily, but then breaks off. In the light winds it is perhaps difficult for either helmsman to gain effective control of the other, and both yachts go for the line at the gun with clear air—*Intrepid *with a slight advantage.*

Intrepid established and maintained a slim lead but was unable to cover her rival effectively. *Courageous* initiated a few tacks as soon as *Intrepid* threatened to attain a blanketing position. Each yacht tacked with agonizing slowness, turning with great majesty, then heading way off the wind to gain speed. About halfway up the first leg, *Intrepid* held to the south just long enough for *Courageous* to slip into a wind shift and get away. When they came together *Intrepid* passed behind *Courageous*'s stern. Both yachts tacked again, and while *Intrepid* had gained considerably, she could not cross *Courageous*—which had the right-of-way—and had to either tack or bear away. *Intrepid* tacked, trying to establish a safe leeward position, but the tactic failed and she fell away far to leeward. That was the race.

Courageous led *Intrepid* all the way around the course and maintained a 3-minute advantage at each mark. The Committee shortened the course to finish downwind, as the race had taken over four hours and the wind was dying. *Intrepid* was catching up, and quite naturally those in her camp claimed that they might have caught *Courageous* on the final beat. In fact, it was highly unlikely, and what little there was to be proven this day was already witnessed.

Aboard Gamecock: *Friday, August 23*
Weather: Hazy, some sun and rain (weak cold front approaching and passing at approximately 1600).

Shortly after the Race Committee starts Courageous *and* Intrepid, *the storm that has been threatening moves into the area causing a*

pages 68–70. *Courageous* performed the difficult jibe-set maneuver to perfection in beating *Mariner* for the last time. Note that spinnaker is set and drawing before the stern has cleared the mark. Such precision teamwork is essential to a successful America's Cup campaign and is developed only after months of practice and training.

wind shift. Courageous *is ahead, although neither yacht now seems to have a particular advantage. The Race Committee halts the race after 3 legs because of the wind shift, with* Courageous *leading by a substantial margin.*

Another start is signaled from the Committee's yacht, Carltina.

Intrepid won the next start, but the postponement signal was hoisted intsead of the starting shape because of another wind shift turning the windward leg into a reach.

Intrepid appeared to win the third start but she had started prematurely. She returned to start properly and thereby threw away her lead and any chance to win the race. Another wind shift also turned this windward leg into a reach, and the race was halted after 2 legs with *Courageous* the winner. The margin was 1 minute, 13 seconds.

Most observers agreed that it had been an inconclusive day. While *Courageous* had picked up two much-needed wins over her wooden rival, they were on technicalities. Still, one had the feeling that the momentum had shifted perceptibly in *Courageous*'s favor. With two yachts so closely matched, it could be that the "psyche factor"—one yacht establishing a winning momentum—would prove decisive. Perhaps this would be the turning point in the match, which everyone assumed at this point would end in *Courageous* being selected even though they conceded that *Intrepid* was a solid sentimental favorite.

Aboard Gamecock: *Saturday, August 24*
Weather: Hazy, followed by dense fog from about 1400 to 1500.
    Wind SW 12–15 knots.

Dennis Conner joined Courageous's *crew today as starting helmsman. Conner had been the most effective starter in whatever Twelve he had been sailing. He offered his services now that* Mariner *and* Valiant *are eliminated, and he was put aboard this morning.*

Courageous, started by Conner, took the lead from the start but led by an extremely slim 10-second margin at the first mark. *Intrepid* appeared to catch up to almost overlap at times on the first reach. *Courageous* had the inside berth at the wing mark after the first reach, but *Intrepid* caught up again to almost overlap at the leeward mark.

At this point the fog became a factor. Both yachts had nearly missed the leeward mark because of diminishing visibility. When the mark appeared out of the fog, it was to starboard—giving *Courageous* the advantage as she jibed over and rounded ahead of *Intrepid* by several boatlengths. Had they been on the opposite side of the mark, *Intrepid* would have had the advantage.

Courageous covered *Intrepid* tack for tack on the upwind leg until both yachts disappeared into dense fog. The race was abandoned a few minutes later.

Aboard Gamecock: *Sunday, August 25*
Weather: Clear. Wind SSW 10 knots.

The start is delayed waiting for wind which finally fills in from the south-southwest just before 1500. Driscoll blows the start, letting Conner beat him by 32 seconds, but Intrepid *hangs onto her rival on the first beat.*

Normally, if two yachts are evenly matched and one gets the lead at the start it will move out on the yacht behind because it has clear wind and the ability to cross the other's wind on each tack. However, *Courageous* was not able to move out on *Intrepid* on this first beat, and the latter appeared to close some of the distance.

Under similar circumstances to the previous day's race, *Intrepid* definitely caught *Courageous* on the first reach and almost passed her, but *Courageous* had the inside position at the reaching mark and was able to hold onto the lead by a very slim margin—perhaps a boatlength. The official time was 13 seconds!

The closest race of the summer and perhaps the most exciting race in all America's Cup trials had *Intrepid* continually threaten *Courageous.* Here *Intrepid* draws even as both yachts approach the reaching mark . . .

. . . but *Courageous* has the inside berth as they jibe around the mark.

Courageous holds off Intrepid and rounds the mark with a boatlength lead.

Again Intrepid threatened on the second reach. She held high, above the course, trying to get by. As they approached the mark, Intrepid pulled up to overlap Courageous, and then she drew almost even. With Intrepid on the inside berth at the third mark, she would move into the lead. There appeared to be nothing Courageous could do to prevent it, but with a dramatic maneuver, Courageous headed up, forcing Intrepid up also. Courageous carried Intrepid beyond the mark—which the rules entitle her to do as long as she also sails above the mark. When Courageous broke off and jibed for the mark, she regained the lead to round 10 seconds ahead of Intrepid.

Intrepid continued to catch up on the second reach, and nearing the leeward mark she overlapped *Courageous* again.

With the inside berth this time, *Intrepid* would surely be able to take the lead.

opposite above. *Courageous* lets go her spinnaker guy preparing to lower the spinnaker.

opposite below. *Intrepid's* spinnaker starts down. *Courageous's* spinnaker is not yet down, and she heads up to take *Intrepid* beyond the mark.

above. Having taken *Intrepid* above the mark and gone above it herself (which she had to do to preclude a protest by *Intrepid*), *Courageous* jibes for the mark.

opposite. *Intrepid* follows . . .

. . . as *Courageous*'s spinnaker
finally comes down on the windward side.

above. *Courageous* rounds, leaving
the mark on her port side as
required, and *Intrepid* follows with
her potential lead and overlap
broken.

Courageous extended her lead to 47 seconds on the second beat—her greatest lead of the day.

On this leg a small red sloop in the spectator fleet blundered onto the course. The spectators had been particularly difficult to control—it was Sunday, good weather, the fleet was large, and the patrol vessels were split between the *France–Southern Cross* race and this one. The red sloop had been cautioned earlier, and it appeared the skipper of the ever-present USCG 42321 had reached the end of his rope. He pulled out of his patrol position, approached the red sloop as soon as the Twelves had passed, ordered the skipper to heave-to, and gave him a summons for sailing in the restricted area. The maximum penalty if convicted, $500!

While the Coast Guard had to do a lot of verbal pushing and shoving, this was the only summons issued all summer. It was the most effective patrol (exasperating for photographers) ever seen on the America's Cup course.

Intrepid gained once again on the run. *Courageous* tried valiantly to hold her off—both yachts jibing for position—*Intrepid* trying to get between *Courageous* and the wind and *Courageous* trying to keep her wind clear. As they approached the mark, *Intrepid* appeared to come almost even, but *Courageous* pulled ahead just before rounding and held the lead, which had dwindled once again to a mere 16 seconds.

Soon after the yachts rounded the last mark, the wind shifted, making it a close reach to the finish. This assured *Courageous* the win. She crossed the finish line with 10 seconds to spare in an anticlimactic finish to the most closely fought race ever seen on the America's Cup course.

pages 80–81. "*Intrepid* gained once again on the run. *Courageous* tried valiantly to hold her off—both yachts jibing for position—*Intrepid* trying to get between *Courageous* and the wind and *Courageous* trying to keep her wind clear."

pages 82–83. "As they approached the mark, *Intrepid* appeared to come almost even, but *Courageous* pulled ahead just before rounding and held the lead, which had dwindled once again to a mere 16 seconds."

Intrepid protested *Courageous* for the maneuver, which carried them both past the third mark, but the Committee disallowed the protest, saying *Courageous* was within her rights to sail both yachts above the mark.

Intrepid flew a new North mainsail for the first time in this race. It was nicknamed "The Frisbee" because it was shaped very full with a leach that curved to windward in light air. Later, I spoke to John Marshall, *Intrepid*'s sail trimmer, who also made the sail, about the Frisbee. "I'm really pleased with it," John told me. "It's very full in light air, and when it breezes up, the leach falls away." It was very nearly a perfect all-weather mainsail, and *Intrepid* not only used hers to good advantage throughout the series, but Marshall also sold one to *Courageous*—although they never raced with it.

Aboard Gamecock: *Tuesday, August 27*
Weather: Cloudy. Wind S 12–15 knots.

This promises to be a pivotal day for Intrepid. *In the previous race* (August 25), *while behind,* Intrepid *continued to threaten* Courageous. *If, in today's race, she can get ahead and then extend her lead it should be extremely significant.*

At the start it seemed that the previous race would be repeated. Everyone expected *Courageous* to be faster in these conditions. *Courageous* won the start although *Intrepid* had clear wind. *Intrepid* took a double tack early in the leg to get out of phase with *Courageous* and break her cover. Gradually *Intrepid* worked up on *Courageous* as they split tacks. When they came together halfway up the leg, it appeared that *Intrepid* might be able to tuck into a safe leeward position, but (according to a later interview with John Marshall) they decided to take one more hitch before forcing the issue. When they crossed again with *Intrepid* on starboard tack, *Courageous* could not cross and was forced to take *Intrepid*'s stern.

It remained to be seen if *Intrepid* could extend the lead. She did. They were 9½ seconds ahead at the first mark, 15 at the reaching mark, 18 at the bottom mark, 40 at the second-weather mark, 33 at the second-bottom mark, and 1 minute, 12 seconds at the finish.

Intrepid's stock rose considerably. Spirits were high on her dock following the race and, while the score stood at 4 for *Courageous* to 2 for *Intrepid*, it was clear that the momentum had swung back to the *Intrepid* camp. She was the yacht to beat again. Another win as impressive as today's and the America's Cup Committee might decide in her favor.

Aboard Gamecock: *Wednesday, August 28*
Weather: Hazy, threatening rain. Wind SW 10–15 knots.

Today is a crucial day for both Intrepid *and* Courageous. *Yesterday's win by* Intrepid *put new life in her camp. Their spirits lifted and they began to believe that there was a chance that* Intrepid *could be selected.*

On the America's Cup course, the first significant happening is the hoisting of the Hood sails on Courageous. *She had been going better with the new Norths, but was beaten yesterday with her North sails by* Intrepid's *Frisbee. Today's return to the Hood sails may have been a rationalization for* Courageous *inasmuch as they were beaten with the Norths and Hood is* Courageous's *upwind helmsman.*

At the start both yachts circled well to leeward of the starting line. With 5 minutes to go they were still at it. This seemed to be a new tactic. It doesn't matter when you break off the tailing attempt if neither yacht can get to the line before the starting signal. Either may break away cleanly from his opponent and, while neither may be in a controlling position, neither one is controlled. If both helmsmen are confident of their yacht's speed, neither needs to control the other, and neither can be forced over the line early.

Both yachts were late at the start, which was taken decisively by *Intrepid.* In a bold maneuver, *Intrepid* tacked from ahead and to leeward of *Courageous* while both were approaching the line on starboard tack. *Intrepid* crossed *Courageous* with half a boatlength to spare. *Courageous* just barely laid the America's Cup buoy—had to pinch slightly to get around, which slowed her a bit more.

Intrepid tacked to cover and cross the line on starboard, and *Courageous* simultaneously tacked onto port. When they crossed, *Intrepid* tacked to cover and *Courageous* tacked away, thereby setting up a balletlike rhythm that was to continue throughout almost all of the three windward legs. *Intrepid* would tack to cover, *Courageous* would tack away. After gathering way for about a minute, *Intrepid* would tack to cover, and *Courageous* would tack away falling under *Intrepid.* As *Intrepid* achieved the ideal covering position, she would tack—thereby completing the cycle with each yacht taking from 50 seconds to 1 minute, 15 seconds between tacks until fetching the weather mark. On the first leg *Courageous* took *Intrepid* to the port-tack lay line, from which position *Intrepid* was able to give *Courageous* about 5 minutes of bad air. *Intrepid*'s lead at the first mark was 21 seconds.

Intrepid won with a lead of 51 seconds.

pages 86–87. Once *Intrepid* moved ahead of *Courageous* she was able to pull out, but only by a very slim margin. *Courageous* threatened on the run—much as *Intrepid* had threatened her on the previous race. However, *Intrepid* was able to stay ahead relatively easily and finished with a margin of 1 minute, 12 seconds.

There is considerable joy in the Intrepid *camp and considerable gloom in* Courageous's. Intrepid *has evened the score over the summer against* Courageous, *and it is beginning to appear that the old wooden yacht has a chance of winning selection after all. If she wins tomorrow and makes it three in a row,* Intrepid *will be in an extremely strong position.*

Aboard Gamecock: *Thursday, August 29*
Weather: Fog, followed by partial clearing. Wind ENE 10–15 knots.

For the first time in three races, Dennis Conner is able to get the start from Gerry Driscoll. Courageous *leads* Intrepid *over the line by 24 seconds. However, this time difference is deceiving, as* Courageous *is on starboard tack.* Intrepid *had tacked before crossing the line, thereby losing many seconds in the maneuver.* Courageous *tacked to cover after crossing the line, losing her time after the official start. The yachts are actually quite a bit closer than the time difference would indicate.*

Courageous covered *Intrepid* tack for tack and *Intrepid* was not able to gain as she had in the earlier days. However, on two occasions, the cover was rather loose. Just before getting to the weather mark *Intrepid* picked up a lift on the port tack and easily crossed ahead of *Courageous*, taking the lead and leading at the weather mark by 1 minute, 1 second. This was a serious tactical blunder on the part of *Courageous*'s afterguard. It cost them a very important race and must surely have cost them a great deal of prestige in the eyes of the America's Cup Committee.

The wind varied in intensity and velocity throughout the race and it appeared that it would be a late day. Particularly since the yachts were delayed leaving the harbor by the fog. *Intrepid* held her lead throughout the balance of the race, although, at one point, *Courageous* got an advantage from a lift similar to the one that put *Intrepid* in the lead, but it was not enough to close the distance. *Intrepid* finished with a lead of 54 seconds and further solidified her position.

Courageous Syndicate Manager Bob McCullough rode in from the race course with the crew aboard *Courageous* and it was obvious from their long faces that there was little happiness aboard. The next morning it was announced that Ted Hood would replace Bob Bavier as skipper. Bavier, who successfully defended the Cup in 1964 after replacing Eric Ridder as *Constellation*'s helmsman, was off the yacht. Now, ten years later, he was to know the keen disappointment that Ridder must have felt when relieved by Bavier. The wheel of fortune had completed its circle.

Somber crew aboard *Courageous* as she comes into Newport Harbor on the afternoon of August 31 after having been defeated by *Intrepid* for the third straight race. Syndicate Manager Bob McCullough sits on the boom while skipper Bob Bavier, in the peaked hat, takes the wheel for the last time. The next morning it was announced that Ted Hood, between Bavier and McCullough, was named to be *Courageous*'s skipper.

Firing Bavier and replacing him with Hood was a desperate attempt to get something going on *Courageous*. Another defeat and it would surely be over. Only four race days remained before the America's Cup Committee had to name a defender.

Aboard Gamecock: *Friday, August 30*
Weather: Cloudy, rain at times, gale warnings. Ahead of a forecast
cold front there are light easterly winds.

Most observers are beginning to believe that the America's Cup Committee will allow the series to go on until the last possible moment even though Intrepid *seems to be piling up significant wins. There is nothing to be lost by keeping the yachts hammering away at each other. If the defender is to be* Intrepid, *her races against* Courageous *are bound to improve her. Everyone in the* Intrepid *group understands this and expects the series to continue through Monday. Similarly, if* Courageous *can give* Intrepid *two or three sound thrashings, further competition will help* Courageous *and give her new skipper that much more opportunity to adjust to his new responsibilities. So, should* Intrepid *win today, it doesn't seem likely that she will be picked—although there surely will be a howl from* Intrepid's *"public" if she wins and the Committee does not decide in her favor.*

There was some speculation last night when gale warnings were reported by the Coast Guard that the yachts might not go out. However, they did, and the race started after a two-hour delay waiting for wind.

Once again, *Courageous*, with Dennis Conner at the helm, took the start from *Intrepid*, but it was a similar situation to that of the previous day. This time the official margin was 35 seconds, but this did not accurately reflect the distance between the yachts.

Courageous held her lead longer than she had the previous day, and it wasn't until the reaching leg that *Intrepid* was able to get past. As the yachts were starting the fourth leg (the second beat) it became apparent that the squall was going to hit with full force. The Race Committee announced over the radio that it was abandoning the race.

Both yachts dropped their sails and were under tow from their respective tenders when the squall hit.

If today's race was not conclusive because of the abandonment and the light winds while they raced, it was another psychological victory for *Intrepid.*

Aboard Gamecock: *Sunday, September 1*
Weather: Sunny. Wind light and variable.

There was no wind yesterday, and since there are only two days left for racing, the yachts were to go out early today in an attempt to get in two races. However, they do not leave until approximately 10:30 and when they arrive on the race course there is very little wind, only very light zephyrs from the north. The Committee postpones the races and then at 14:15 abandons racing for the day.

This was certainly an unexpected turn of events, because everyone felt that the Committee would stay out as long as possible and, in fact, about 15 minutes after the racing was abandoned, a nice breeze came up from the southwest. Sunny Vynne, manager of the *Intrepid* Syndicate, thought that perhaps the Committee had decided that they would announce that *Intrepid* would defend the Cup. But an hour and a half after *Intrepid* hit the dock the Committee had not appeared.

After coming in from the race course, *Courageous* went out checking sails. She put up three spinnakers in quick succession going out of the harbor and then went up Narragansett Bay and continued sail testing until late in the afternoon. It was as if they were seeking a magic potion that would fire them with the speed to beat *Intrepid.*

Thus, only one day remained, and if no races could be held on Monday, the America's Cup Committee would have to make a selection on the basis of the score as it stood. Technically, it was even at four each for the final trials and tipped in *Intrepid*'s favor over the summer at 11 to 8. In addition, some of *Courageous*'s wins over *Intrepid* in the final trials were helped by lucky breaks, whereas *Intrepid*'s victories were won the hard way.

Nevertheless, *Courageous* remained the favorite. Most observers believed that if the yachts ended up even, *Courageous* would get the nod, because she was newer and theoretically faster. A very important factor was Olin Stephens' insistence that *Courageous* was the faster yacht and his complete dedication to its syndicate's effort. As the designer of both yachts he had no ax to grind and was in the best position to know the theoretical advantages of each. Therefore, Stephens' continued insistence that *Courageous* had the greater potential must have weighed heavily on the Committee to hold off making a selection.

On the morning of September 2, a CBS radio report stated that whichever yacht won this final race would defend the America's Cup. This was an oversimplification, but it turned out to be accurate. Personally, trying to put myself in the Committee's position, I felt that *Intrepid* ought to be selected. Their effort was unified and their yacht was in perfect tune. They were at the peak of their efficiency. Conversely, *Courageous* was still looking for the key to unlock her potential. The bell would ring at noon in a day and a half, and her new skipper had yet to command a completed race. *Courageous* might have more ultimate potential than *Intrepid*, but it was already past the time when it should have been realized.

Aboard Gamecock: *Monday, September 2—Labor Day*
Weather: Overcast with occasional rain. Wind 15–20 knots from the
NNE, building later to 25 knots.

As Courageous *and* Intrepid *leave the harbor this morning, the* Courageous *backers seem to excel in horn power. This was not the case previously. It is as if by blowing furiously they can provide* Courageous *with the momentum needed to put her, finally, ahead of her rival.*

Outside, at the America's Cup Buoy, the wind was from the northeast between 15 and 18 knots with occasional gusts to 20. *Intrepid* and *Courageous* avoided each other at the start. (Both skippers said later that they were afraid to get into tight maneuvering because in the heavy seas either yacht could get out of control temporarily and collide with the other.) This was no time to take unnecessary chances.

Both yachts started about a minute late, and they couldn't have been farther apart. They were at the extreme opposite ends of the line on opposite tacks—*Courageous* at the Committee boat end on port tack, *Intrepid* at the pin end on starboard.

Courageous tacked to starboard, and *Intrepid* tacked underneath her—appearing to squeeze *Courageous* out. *Courageous* tacked away, and *Intrepid* covered.

Suddenly, *Intrepid* straightened up—heeling less—and a man appeared aloft at the lower spreaders. A few minutes later, *Courageous* tacked for the mark, crossing *Intrepid*. *Intrepid* held on a bit further and, when they squared away for the mark, it was obvious that both yachts had overstood. *Courageous* led by 46 seconds at the first mark and was never threatened thereafter.

Intrepid could not catch up in the heavy conditions. Her crew tried to split jibes reaching high on starboard after *Courageous* had made a beautifully executed jibe set at the beginning of the run. Dennis Conner, *Courageous*'s tactician, and Halsey Herreshoff, her navigator, had called it perfectly. *Courageous* sailed dead downwind straight to the mark and put additional distance between herself and *Intrepid*.

At the finish *Courageous* was ahead by 1 minute, 47 seconds—her most impressive win over *Intrepid* all summer.

A very polite and efficient crew from USCG 42321, captained by Lieutenant David Hosmer, drops Gamecock *on her mooring in Newport Harbor. The yachts have already docked and we leap into the skiff, leaving towline and fenders dangling over* Gamecock's *sides —very unseamanlike!*

As we approach the dock it appears that Navette *is going to* Courageous *first. Could it be that they have picked* Intrepid *after today's defeat? Alas, we have missed* Navette's *visit to* Intrepid. *She has gone there first and is coming to tell* Courageous *that she has been selected to defend the Cup.*

Intrepid had broken her port lower running backstay on the first windward leg. It had appeared that she was slightly ahead at that

time, but as both yachts were quite far apart it was impossible to tell
accurately which was ahead. John Marshall said, following the race,
that the stay parted with such force that he thought surely the mast
would fail. It didn't, but the loose end of the stay had whipped around
the lower spreader. Andy McGowan was hoisted aloft in the bosun's
chair and cleared the stay in a remarkably short time. The broken
ends were fished together with two clamps and *Intrepid* was back in
business in a few minutes. They were not able to exert as much control over the rig as they would have wished in those rough conditions
and it can be assumed—although the crew later made light of the
incident—that the failure may have cost *Intrepid* the race and the
series.

I asked a tearful John Marshall if it had made a difference between winning and losing. At first he wouldn't commit himself, then
he said, rather testily, "Sure it made a difference, whether it made
us . . . you know . . ." Tactician and alternate helmsman, Bill Buchan,
was emphatic that it had made no difference—that they had lost
because *Courageous* had sailed better and faster. It was as if the
Intrepid crew had agreed among themselves that they would not use
a broken wire as an excuse for losing this crucial final race. If so, it
was a grand gesture.

Courageous had won decisively; she would defend the Cup.

Dennis Conner did not start *Courageous* in this race. It was
decided before the start that Ted Hood should sail, because Conner
had never steered a 12-Meter under such rough conditions. Hood had
the helm the entire race and called all the shots. In his first race as
skipper he was able to bring all the pieces together and forge *Courageous* into a winner.

An entire summer of intense competition was condensed into a
single day. A whole summer's work, a dedicated life style for the losers
brought to an abrupt end like turning off a switch: click, nothing. For
the winners it was a time of jubilation and anticipation of the main
event to follow. In a week's time, *Courageous* and *Southern Cross*
would meet on the same waters in Rhode Island Sound. A few minutes after the start of that first race it should be apparent if the New
York Yacht Club's preparation has been sufficient to meet the Aussies'
challenge.

But *Intrepid*'s defeat was not without its compensations. As bitter as their disappointment was, they were to know that it was their effort that had pushed *Courageous* to greater heights than she would have achieved alone.

When the two crews got together on *Courageous*'s dock to congratulate each other, Syndicate Manager Bob McCullough told Gerry Driscoll, "Boy, without you guys, I don't know . . ."

And later McCullough said, "Without *Intrepid*, we would have been sitting ducks for the Australians."

Summing up this final race in *The New York Times*, Steve Cady wrote, ". . . The Americans closed ranks in less than an hour. Eustace (Sunny) Vynne, Jr., the *Intrepid*'s syndicate manager, was asking McCullough what the *Intrepids* could do to help and McCullough was suggesting more tune-up tests between the two boats.

" 'One thing we want to make clear,' said Vynne. 'We got a fair shake from the New York Yacht Club. They couldn't have been fairer.' "

All smiles, but only two are happy. Gerry Driscoll (left) congratulates Bob McCullough (center) and Ted Hood (right) after announcement that *Courageous* will defend the America's Cup.

PRESSURE

The America's Cup has never been won in the sense that a challenger has never been able to wrest the Cup from the defenders. The defenders don't really win it, because they already have it; they just get to keep it for another three or four years until it's time to meet a new challenger. It is believed to be the oldest record in all of sports, a 123-year winning streak.

10

The America's Cup eventually must be lost. The record cannot go on forever. Sooner or later some combination of challenger skill and defender ineptitude will result in a challenger winning the America's Cup. It is said both in jest and to emphasize the magnitude of the disaster that the head of the losing skipper will be mounted in the Trophy Room of the New York Yacht Club in the glass case from which the America's Cup will be taken.

There is tremendous pressure on the defending skipper and crew and each time the Cup is successfully defended the pressure of the next series mounts. When the Cup is finally lost it will not be because the New York Yacht Club was unable to come up with a design or sailing skills sufficient to meet the challenger but because the pressure became too great. Like a festering sore the Cup will one day burst from the doors of the clubhouse on 44th Street. When it does it will be a great relief to some, but to the losing helmsman it will be a pain perhaps too excruciating to endure. It will mean failure—the failure of letting down those who have counted on him. It will be the end of a brilliant sailing career, for the stigma will always follow him. The accusing finger points, "That's the man who lost the America's Cup," and he will turn up his collar, slink down the alley to kick a beer can and spit back at a snarling cat.

Harold Vanderbilt knew the taste of impending defeat in 1934. His defending J Boat, *Rainbow*, was down two races to none to the English challenger, *Endeavour*. In the third race, halfway down the last leg of the triangular course, Vanderbilt was behind and it seemed impossible that they could catch up. In despair he turned the helm over to his tactician, Sherman Hoyt, and it is said that he retired below to write his apologies to the New York Yacht Club for his failure. What thoughts were going through Vanderbilt's mind during those agonizing minutes before the finish can only be guessed. They could not have been pleasant ones.

Fortunately, a combination of skill and determination on Sherman Hoyt's part and a good bit of luck with the weather saved this race, and subsequently, Vanderbilt, Hoyt, and *Rainbow* went on to win the next three races and save the Cup by a score of 4 to 2. It was the closest series in the Cup's history. Harold Vanderbilt was the only man ever to approach the possibility of an America's Cup defeat. Lots of people in sports have known bitter defeat, but the one who gets saddled with this one is going to have something especially difficult to handle.

To be chosen to defend the America's Cup must be one of the greatest achievements to which any U.S. sailor could aspire. Yet it cannot be everyone's bag. Reflect for a moment on the possibilities of being so chosen. Assuming that you had the necessary requisites, were confident enough in your ability, and had the experience to be chosen, would you accept? Would you put your reputation on the line just for the glory of being the twenty-second helmsman to successfully

Pressure

defend the Cup? How does that weigh against the possibility of being the first dummy to lose it?

At the end of the monumental *Intrepid-Courageous* series, after *Mariner* and *Valiant* were both out of it, I asked Ted Turner what his feelings were about America's Cup racing.

"Anyone who says this is a candy-ass league doesn't know what he's talking about," said Turner. "This was the toughest summer ever. You work hard, you don't make the grade, you let a lot of your friends down."

"I enjoy sailing,' Turner continued, "that's why I do it. But, man, this summer wasn't any fun at all!"

Turner was really down at that time. He had been through the wringer. People said he was talking to himself, indicating that it was a sign that he was cracking under the pressure. Turner didn't crack—he always talks to himself. That's the way he relieves his pressures. Nevertheless, there was no questioning the fact that Ted Turner—World Ocean Racing Champion, Southern Ocean Racing Conference Champion, 5.5-Meter World Champion, Gold Cup Champion, North American Flying Dutchman Champion, Transatlantic Race winner, Fastnet Race winner, Sydney-Hobart Race winner—had never been under the kind of strain the America's Cup elimination trials placed upon him. When *Mariner* and *Valiant* were eliminated, Turner was a beaten man—not only beaten on the race course, but beaten spiritually as well.

Fortunately, Turner doesn't stay beaten. I happened to run into Ted outside The Candy Store on Friday the thirteenth during the Cup Races. Ted had two lovely young women with him. One was Laurie Dayton, the daughter of Assistant Syndicate Manager Duke Dayton, and the other was the friend of another crew member.

"Hey, Jonesy," was Turner's greeting, "how do you get into The Candy Store? I've never been here before and I'd like to buy these lovely girls a drink. Why don't you join us?"

I did a quick aboutface and in we went.

Ted obviously had recovered some of his normally abundant self-confidence. In view of his earlier feelings I asked him if he would ever consider doing the America's Cup again. "Yes, I would do it again," he said, "but not with Britton Chance. I'd like to buy *Courageous*, that would be the only way to go. Doing a new boat is too much trouble—it takes too much time [pronounced 'tahm' in his Atlanta drawl] to get a new boat goin'. I'd like to race against Dennis Conner next time and beat his ass."

In talking with Laurie, I got the impression that time had healed some of the wounds in the *Mariner* camp. Turner particularly was highly regarded—not to say the hero of the summer. He had held the thing together from the beginning. When it was first obvious that *Mariner* was not the boat they had hoped she'd be, everyone wanted to quit, to get off the boat and go, but Turner wouldn't let them. Even when he was relieved as *Mariner*'s skipper, he wouldn't let his crew come with him on *Valiant*. Laurie's father, Duke Dayton, told me several days later that Ted had talked to his crew, telling them that even though they might feel that they should quit out of loyalty to him, they should stay with *Mariner*. According to Dayton, Turner had told them, "We came here to defend the Cup. Anyone who quits now will never sail with me again."

I got the same thing from seventeen-year-old Rusty Dayton, who sailed aboard *Mariner*. He came up to our table to borrow five dollars from his sister. As Rusty bounded gleefully into a night of adventure, clutching the fiver, he indicated Turner and said, "What a good guy!"

Don't be surprised if we see Ted Turner and the Dayton clan back in action together for the next challenge.

I'm sure not everyone has the same warm feelings about Turner that the Daytons exhibited. The great difficulty with a losing America's Cup effort is that people get desperate. The worse things get, the more everyone looks for someone or something to blame. Tempers flare, angry words are spoken. It gets to everyone. Everyone is to blame. In the *Mariner* case Turner probably came out bigger than anyone else in the eyes of most of his shipmates, but he still had a long way to go before getting back the self-confidence with which he began the summer. *And Turner's side won!*

"Twelve-Meter racing is a tremendously high-pressure operation," according to John Marshall, *Intrepid* sail trimmer. "There is no room for second place. As a result, the tensions are nearly unbearable and a well-integrated cohesive group that can function well under these conditions day after day, living together for an entire summer, without developing frictions or animosities, is essential."

Even among successful crews—those who win their selection trials and go on to defend the Cup—the pressure sometimes is not worth the sacrifices that must be made. I have friends who have sailed

A blurry Ted Turner toasts to defeat in the downstairs porch bar of The Candy Store. "I'd like to race against Dennis Conner next time and beat his ass."

in defenders in previous years. Most of them treasure their experience and have benefited from it. Some, however, while not exactly sorry that they did it, came away with scars that will never fade. Some gave up careers that might have been enhanced by their participation in the America's Cup but somehow weren't. Others lost long-standing friendships to the pressures of the campaign—successful though it was. One even lost his love of the sport. Once an enthusiastic and experienced offshore and one-design sailor, after spending his third summer on a Cup defender, he gave up competitive sailing altogether.

In the words of Duncan Spencer, racing in the America's Cup is "an act on which a whole lifetime may be judged."*

* "Cup Focus" by Bob Fisher, *Yachts & Yachting*, November 1, 1974, p. 1044.

The pressures facing the skipper of the challenger may be just as great or even greater than those facing the defending skipper, but they are of a very different sort. There is a great deal less to lose. Win, and you have done what no man has been able to do for twelve decades! Lose, and you join the increasingly larger group of those who have tried valiantly and not made it. Even to lose, but to have put up a strong fight, to have beaten the defender in one race, to have threatened him in others, as Jim Hardy did in *Gretel II* in 1970, is to do better than other men in similar circumstances have been able to do.

Somewhat more than the defender, the challenger carries with him the national pride of his countrymen, particularly in the case of the Australian challengers, whose skippers and crew members represent an Australian sports mania. Like the losers in the Roman Colosseum—when Australians lose, a nation turns thumbs down on the lot.

AMERICA'S CUP PEOPLE

11

So much fuss is made over the latest equipment, sails, and hull designs of the 12-Meters in an America's Cup series that people tend to forget that there are real people involved. If an America's Cup series makes for good boat watching, it is even better for people watching.

America's Cup people come in a great variety of types, sizes, and shapes. First come the crew members—young, muscular, good-looking chaps who come from all over the world like ancient gladiators to do battle for honor and country. Anywhere one finds such young men one also finds young, good-looking, friendly women—be they wives, sweethearts, or independents (hoping, perhaps, to become one of the former)—strolling the streets of Newport, sunning themselves aboard the spectator craft, or sipping tall, cool drinks on the porch of The Candy Store.

The first two categories could get nowhere, of course, without the wealthy financiers who make up the syndicates who own the Twelves. They and their friends add much color and class—if not much excitement—to the proceedings. Akin to the last mentioned, but aloof, are the stuffy (and not so stuffy) Committee members and other officials who are seen only infrequently but are, nevertheless, a vital addition to the scene.

There are numerous members of the "fourth estate" who have come to report on proceedings. They range from the bearded Kiwi from Boston to the barrel-gutted Limey from the *Guardian* who are Commodore and Vice-Commodore of SINS (Society of International Nautical Scribes).

Finally, there are the America's Cup fans—definitely not the beer-drinking undershirt crowd one sees at the ballpark, but so diverse as to defy description. Definitely, America's Cup time is people watching at its best.

A stroll from Port O'Call down what used to be Pelham Street past the Black Pearl, the Cinzano umbrellas of the outdoor bar, over the cobblestones and past the shops of Bowen's Wharf will most likely bring one face to face with a variety of America's Cup people, some of whom you will no doubt meet.

"ANONYMOUS"

In a town like Newport during an America's Cup, where there are plenty of bars and plenty of nighttime action, there are plenty of people looking for it and more people looking for it than finding it. Such was the case with an executive-type friend who was on the scene to see a race or two and incidentally looking for someone with whom to share an evening. He was complaining bitterly about the lack of opportunity and his singular lack of success, but we left him sitting with a young woman as we went off to dinner. He would most likely join us later, he said, but of course he didn't. We saw him late the same evening at The Candy Store. He was with the same woman, working hard to score and not looking like he was getting anywhere. I saw him the next day and asked how he made out.

"I was very lucky, yes sir, very lucky." He said, "You know, I eventually went home with that girl and there were three others living in the same apartment, all of them gorgeous airline stewardesses, and the other three were complaining about there being no action!"

"RELUCTANT HELMSMAN"

On Sunday, September 1, William N. Wallace wrote in *The New York Times* that it was ironic that Ted Hood was in Newport at all. Unfortunately, this was the last line in Wallace's piece and it must have puzzled his readers. What fell on the cutting-room floor of *The Times* was the explanation that Hood had planned to spend the summer in England campaigning his new One Ton Cup yacht, *Robin*, in the World One Ton series. *Robin* had been loaded on a freighter in June and was bound for England when the freighter developed propeller problems and returned to port with *Robin* still on her deck. Time ran out before other arrangements could be made.

Hood found himself in Newport early in July, and he was asked to go out on *Courageous* as he had throughout the spring to help tune the sails his company had made. Feeling they had much to learn from Ted Hood, the *Courageous* people asked permission of the America's Cup Committee to carry twelve crew members instead of the eleven maximum allowed for the July trials. Hood sailed every day as an extra crew member, which rather irritated the *Intrepid* group. However, the *Courageous* Syndicate had asked for and received permission in advance; there was nothing *Intrepid* could do about it.

During the July trials *Courageous* continued to have problems, but Hood's valuable contribution to making her go fast began to tell and she showed decided improvement. The logical conclusion was that Hood should become a permanent member of the crew and he stepped officially into the cockpit as relief helmsman to Bob Bavier for the final trials in August.

Hood was not overjoyed by this turn of events. He had been asked earlier to skipper *Courageous* and had turned the job down. He was openly critical of her layout, her two steering wheels, and as a designer he would much rather have sailed his own 12-Meter—which he had done with *Nefertiti* in 1962 and 1964.

Frederick E. (Ted) Hood could be described as the complete sailor. He grew up in Marblehead, Massachusetts, sailing a great variety of boats and then, after World War II, with his father's technical assistance he established Hood Sailmakers. One of the principal differences between Hood sails and others was that Hood manufactured his own sailcloth. Not content with the lack of tightness of the weave that was available from commercial looms, Hood set up his own looms to weave his own cloth where he could control the weave, providing cloth very much more tightly woven than those made on commercial looms. The tighter weave produced a superior sailcloth. Hood Sailmakers has grown to the point where it is a part of a large conglomerate, and there are Hood lofts in major sailing areas all over the world.

Having established himself as a sailmaker, Hood turned to yacht design and his first yacht was for himself, a 40-foot centerboard yawl, *Robin*, which proved very successful in a summer's racing. Hood sold her at the end of the season and proceeded immediately to design and build another yacht. A procession of *Robin*s, *Robin Too*'s, and *Robin Two Too*'s followed, from 34 to 56 feet, so many that Hood himself has lost track. Hood designed the 12-Meter *Nefertiti* in 1962. *Nefertiti* was a very radical departure from current 12-Meter thinking. She was primarily a heavy-weather boat and excelled under those conditions. However, she was weak in light and moderate air and with Hood at the helm with Hood sails on her spars, *Nefertiti* was runnerup in the selection series in which the America's Cup Committee picked Bus Mosbacher's *Weatherly*. Since 1962 Hood sails have been the standard on virtually all the 12-Meters in contention to defend the Cup. Both North and Hard sails made an appearance in Cup racing in 1970 but Hood's still proved superior and have defended the America's Cup every year since 1958. It was quite natural then that Hood sails should be aboard *Courageous* in the initial stages of the series and also natural for Hood to be involved with *Courageous* and her crew getting the most out of them.

But it was the merest chance that brought Hood to become a permanent crew member aboard *Courageous*. This chance was the breakdown of the freighter that failed to take his One-Tonner to England.

As talented as Hood is in so many departments, he is not noted for his tactical ability on the starting line. *Courageous* continued to prove weak in that area well into the final trials, and when *Mariner* was eliminated, her helmsman, Dennis Conner, was picked by the *Courageous* Syndicate to come aboard and act as starting helmsman.

Very soon it developed that Conner would start *Courageous*, Hood would sail it upwind, and Bavier would steer downwind. Such an arrangement with three helmsmen was not viable. When *Courageous* continued to lose and it appeared that, in fact, *Intrepid* would be selected to defend the Cup, Bavier stepped down as skipper and the syndicate appointed Ted Hood to be skipper with Dennis Conner still to be starting helmsman and tactician. This was clearly an eleventh-hour desperation move, but it was perhaps the key that *Courageous* had been looking for all summer. With what turned out to be only one race left before selection had to be made, *Courageous*, under Hood's command, put it all together.

Hood's summer was not without its anguish. *Intrepid* had been winning earlier in the season with North sails, with North's East Coast sailmaker, John Marshall, in her afterguard. It appeared that the Hood monopoly in 12-Meter sails was being broken. The genoas, mains, and spinnakers all were excellent and, sailing with them, *Intrepid* was difficult, if not impossible, to beat. Leaving no stone unturned, the *Courageous* Syndicate ordered a suit of North sails early in July and *Courageous* came to the line with Ted Hood trimming North sails in the final trials. This is not the sort of thing that bothers Hood, but the president of his company was quietly tearing his hair in Marblehead at the thought. Not only were North sails aboard *Courageous* but Ted Hood himself was having to sail with them.

"... he commands universal respect among those who sail with him ..."

On that last day Hood steered *Courageous* through the entire race. Dennis Conner did not start, and they used Hood mainsail and genoa. Hood proved to be the catalyst needed to develop *Courageous*'s true potential.

For all his many abilities, Ted Hood remains a shy and very quiet man. He rarely raises his voice to his crew, and perhaps because of his quietness and the innate ability, which is easily recognized, he commands universal respect among those who sail with him. It is not because of selfishness that Hood's vast storehouse of sailing knowledge remains pretty much within his own head but because of his quietness, which prevades all his associations. When asked even detailed and lengthy questions Hood's response is likely to be "yes," "no," "probably," or "I don't think so." An interview with Ted Hood sounds more like an interrogation in a court of law. And the interviewer must be particularly skillful if he is to bring forth any worthwhile commentary.

THE "BOSUN"

Andy McGowan was the "bosun" aboard *Intrepid*. The rigging, winches, spars, and all the items that make the sails work were his special responsibility. Each day at 0800 Andy could be seen up *Intrepid*'s mast inspecting the rig and fittings, wiping the moisture off the spar, or perhaps making some adjustment or part replacement. After sailing all day—either practicing or racing—you'd likely find Andy up the mast again kicking at a recalcitrant halyard lock or making a fine adjustment late in the day just before *Intrepid* would be hauled out of the water on her special hoist.

Andy is a naval architect with Sparkman & Stephens, the designers of both *Intrepid* and *Courageous*, and was involved with *Intrepid*'s redesign for this series. His primary experience has been in ocean racing, having (at age twenty-six) put together a group to campaign a One Ton Class yacht in both the North American and World championships, and having sailed many hundreds of miles aboard *Charisma*, one of the most successful large U.S. ocean racers. He was one of only two of *Intrepid*'s crew not from the West Coast (the other being John Marshall).

It was a tough summer for McGowan, a summer of hard work, and conscientious attention to minute details, and it all ended with a

bang as one of his lovingly cared-for wires let go at the most inopportune time imaginable. Andy was up the mast in a flash, but the damage had been done. His summer came to an abrupt and unexpected end, surely worthwhile but ultimately a disappointment.

THE "BRIGHTWORK QUEEN"

"Kiwi Jill" is typical of a type one sees in almost any boating community who catches rides from Bora Bora to the Galapagos with whoever will have them aboard. They do not have boats of their own, but they love to sail and are ready to go wherever the winds take them, whenever anyone will take them. "Boat bum" is the common term applied to these people, but it is unfairly uncomplimentary to most—even if it is descriptive. Whatever the term, the description fits Jill. Her inquisitive, dancing brown eyes twinkled as they delighted in telling about the sights they had seen in the Mediterranean, the Caribbean, and the South Pacific aboard a great variety of cruising yachts. Mostly Jill cooks and she confessed that at times when she is called on deck to give a hand, she's either forgotten the name of the line she's asked to trim or else she is unfamiliar with the nautical terminology of the country from which her host's yacht hails. She loves to sail, but the crewing is perhaps better left to others.

Jill wore her long red hair piled loosely on top of her head or draped casually over bare, brown shoulders. A favorite outfit was a pinkish-brown halter top, fastened around her neck with a loop of wire, which accentuated her enticingly unencumbered breasts. While she was often seen in The Candy Store, she said she preferred less crowded places.

"Everyone's always grabbing and pinching," she said of the crowds in the bars, and it was easy to understand the temptation. Men find her extremely attractive.

Jill wasn't able to sail enough over the summer, but she liked the scene at Newport. She hired out as a free-lance varnisher—refinishing the brightwork on several well-known yachts—to earn enough money to stay all summer. Later she took a job as cook aboard one of the large power yachts in order to see the final trials and the Cup races. Then it would be off to some place warmer. Florida? the Bahamas? the Virgin Islands? Anyone looking for a crew with dancing brown eyes?

"INTREPID WIFE"

(by Mike Levitt)

The old line goes, "Behind every great man there is a great woman." Whether true or not, behind the *Intrepid* effort there was an inordinate number of great women as the "People's Boat" attracted an abundance of beautiful people. While the eyes of the West Coast followed *Intrepid*, the eyes of Newport were on the *Intrepid* "golden girls," be they wives, friends, or camp followers. The *Intrepid* camp had the ambiance of a college football game. For the *Intrepid* fans, the America's Cup was a sailing Rosebowl resplendent with boat horns sounded in either victory or defeat; large crowds lining the dock at

Williams & Manchester Shipyard—often waiting well into the night for a glimpse of the yacht, crew, and, of course, the cheerleaders.

Pearl Necklace was the flagship of the *Intrepid* camp. Those aboard were either syndicate dignitaries, especially invited reporters (such as Mike Levitt, Associate Editor of *Yacht Racing* magazine, who kindly contributed this most attractive bit of *Intrepid* color), or they represented the inner circle of wives, girlfriends, or friends of girlfriends. A more enthusiastic or lovely group of cheerleaders would be hard to imagine. It was difficult, even for the most cynical reporter, not to get caught up in the spirit of *Intrepid*.

The unofficial head cheerleader of this ad hoc squad was Judy Koch, whose husband Steve worked deep in the bowels of *Intrepid*, grinding the port winch. Judy has the apple-pie kind of good looks that it would be un-American not to like. A former Cole of California bathing-suit model and now first-grade teacher in Mercer Island, Washington, the long-legged, well-tanned Judy is the kind of teacher who makes you want to go back to school.

With the June, July, and August vacation, unique to teachers or the very rich, Judy was a mainstay of the *Pearl Necklace* gang. She possessed a combination of warmth, enthusiasm, and beauty that both people and cameras gravitate to. Not only did she have the look of sunshine, but she tended to speak in that "silver-lining" sunny way, with an abundance of bright exclamation points.

Providing an overview of the summer, Judy said, "I wouldn't have traded one minute of it for anything. As I look back, it was great! We met so many fine people and made some lasting friendships. Everyone made us feel so welcome and the enthusiastic well-wishers

Intrepid's "Golden Girl" Judy Koch. (Mike Levitt photo)

Intrepid's cheerleaders in action. (Mike Levitt photo)

at home were inspirational. We were celebrities for the moment, with whom everyone wanted to trade places, and for the most part we loved it."

After returning home Judy reflected on her summer. "The pressures of such an intense existence were far from always being pleasant. Selfishly, I am thankful to have my husband to myself again and am thoroughly enjoying the privacy of our own home and the freedom to be *me* again, rather than an *Intrepid* wife. It was not easy to be jerked from a life where one lives by his own rules and makes his own decisions and placed in a situation similar to pledging a fraternity. It's hard to live in a manner someone else decides is best. It is equally difficult to spend three months with only a few moments (if any) to be alone with your mate. It is awkward to have to talk in whispers, tiptoe down hallways, and be afraid of waking someone if you flush the head after 10:00 P.M. It's not the greatest to have to put on an evening dress (or coat and tie) after bobbing on the ocean for twelve hours when it has been 90-degree weather with winds gusting to two knots. Nor is it fun to only be able to iron or use the laundry after 9:30 P.M. (along with ten others)—or not to play the piano after dinner—or eat breakfast at 7:00 A.M.—or be the sixth one in line for the shower when dinner is served in fifteen minutes—or ride your bike ten blocks to the store for toothpaste when you're still recovering from falling off the day before! It wasn't neat to find your husband had to leave on business during one of the two short breaks all summer—or having to tell your friends and family that after coming two thousand miles across the country there just wasn't room for them on the tender—or being thrown from side to side in five-foot waves on a fishing tug while struggling to watch a race—or trying to stay awake after taking a pill (which makes you drowsy) for seasickness so you can save face among the more seaworthy observers. There *were* some drawbacks. It's not the kind of thing you'd sign up for again next summer. It's great to be home—even though the Skagit Head Race is this weekend and Steve just *has* to defend his trophy. So it begins again. . . .

"But there was real Western Spirit in the *Intrepid* camp, and I haven't seen the likes of it anywhere for a long while. We were proud to represent the greatest part of the U.S. Newport, the New York Y.C. and the entire East Coast will long remember, 'Knock on Wood.' *Intrepid*, hip-hip hooray!!"

"COURAGEOUS BALLERINA"

Intrepid wasn't the only 12-Meter to have an attractive entourage. *Courageous* had her share as well, and one such pretty *Courageous* fan was Tara Ann Nicholson.

Tara Ann was finishing out her first year at Wheaton College when she visited a friend in Newport over Easter vacation. Her friend's sister was looking for a roommate for the summer—which sounded like a good opportunity if Tara could find a job. Christie's Restaurant hired her as a waitress, but she was laid off. After a couple of interim jobs—helping get Castle Hill ready for the French and filling in for a vacationing receptionist (whose boss is the Commodore of the local Ida Lewis Yacht Club), Tara Ann got a more permanent job as a waitress at the Black Pearl.

Shuttling between the tables on the terrace overlooking Bowen's Wharf and The Pearl's kitchen on the other side of West Pelham Street, Tara Ann eventually met everyone in Newport.

Tara Ann was not a typical college woman. Although only twenty, she studied ballet for fifteen years and danced professionally before deciding to give up her career and go to college. Hardly the narrow sort of person one might expect would come out of such an intense background, it is probably safe to assume that Tara Ann captivated everyone fortunate enough to meet her with her warmth and unabashed friendliness.

Tara Ann met a particular *Courageous* crew member in June "but was busy having a rowdy time and dating other people," she said. "It wasn't long before I was meeting all kinds of interesting people and attending the various functions and parties."

Courageous cheerleaders: "Go 'Rageous!" Tara Ann and her friend Dawn Winston.

Tara and her *Courageous* friend began dating at the end of June and they were steady company (when he wasn't sailing and she wasn't working) for almost the entire summer.

"As a result, I became more involved with the races," said Tara, "learned much more about sailing, and became good friends with other guys on the *Courageous* crew."

While most people were rooting for *Intrepid*, Tara Ann remained a steadfast *Courageous* fan. As unpopular as this position could be, she hung on through *Courageous*'s darkest hours and was duly rewarded—ending the summer with an "I told you so" grin that could have made Gerry Driscoll and Jim Hardy happy they had lost.

Unfortunately, Wheaton beckoned before the America's Cup series began, but she was back for the windup of the series and in on the victory celebrations for her favorite 12-Meter. Classes be damned, Newport was too strong a magnet to resist, especially when Wheaton was only a couple of hours away.

It is not too difficult to appreciate that Tara Ann Nicholson could be a principal attraction to many who hung around The Black Pearl, the Twelves, and Newport, but what was the nature of the magnet that drew Tara Ann to Newport and caused her to regard her twentieth summer as something very special? To Tara, "Newport is a feeling, a memory like an Indian summer day in October that we savor because it will be a long time before it comes again. It's a fairytale that becomes a part of our childhood, regardless of how old we are. It's a hundred people that love the harbor's sunset when the Twelves come home who now are somewhere else watching another sunset. It's throwing your head back with joy when your favorite boat wins. It's drinking champagne. It's unending energy and few sleeping hours. It's people. . . ."

It's surely people like Tara Ann Nicholson.

THE PRESS

Most big-city newspapers have discovered the America's Cup and provide coverage of the match itself. A few have become enlightened by interested staff people who have somehow promoted a summer's duty in Newport to cover the trials *and* the America's Cup match. Good duty for the reporter who can wangle it.

Washington, D.C., is blessed with two well-known dailies—*The*

Washington Post and *The Star-News*—and both were represented by on-the-scene-all-summer reporters who had gathered unto themselves this plum of an assignment. Nor was this the first America's Cup for *The Post*'s Judy Lawson or *The Star-News*'s Duncan Spencer—both have been regulars for a couple of America's Cup series.

Judy and Duncan were often aboard *Gamecock* for the trials. Both were aboard the final day and shared the ignominy of our long tow behind USCG 42321 from the race course back to Newport. In fact, it was Duncan who diagnosed the nature of *Gamecock*'s "illness" and effected repairs to her ailing fuel pump the next day.

DUNCAN SPENCER

While a summer at Newport would be pure fun for most people, for Duncan Spencer it was work—not that he complained at all, but he surely was busy all the time, talking with the French or Australians, trying to get something out of a syndicate spokesman, or cornering one of the helmsmen to get a story. One would see Duncan with his battered Aussie cap, knobby knees sticking out below his tan Bermuda shorts, pencil poised above a waterlogged spiral binder while his steely blue eyes pierced the gaze of his interviewee.

Spencer lived a far different life in Newport from that of most America's Cup followers aboard *Karin*, a 52-foot German-built sloop belonging to his father. A typical day would begin after breakfast with a row ashore to catch a boat ride out to the race course. After spending all day on the water, he would dash ashore to whichever dock promised the best story, then retire to the press headquarters at the Armory to write and phone in his story. With a little luck he'd get a

Duncan Spencer is the only person in the world who can see anything through his binoculars.

late evening beer at a bar down Thames Street before rowing back to *Karin* to cook supper and go to bed. Duncan's view was definitely not from The Candy Store (I don't think I ever saw him there) but from a press boat, shipyard dock, or looking backward over the oars of *Karin*'s seven-foot, nine-inch Dhow dinghy—his mode of transportation from home to place of business.

Duncan received periodic visits from his architect wife and inquisitive children who shared *Karin*'s comfortable accommodations for a weekend, but mostly his life in Newport was one of observer, scribe, dinghy rower, and ace mechanic—an unusual life by the standards set around him.

JUDY LAWSON

Judy Lawson's daily activities paralleled Duncan Spencer's except she lived ashore like conventional folks. Judy is one of the top woman sailors in the United States, and is probably the most knowledgeable, in sailing matters, of the U.S. daily press reporters. Like Duncan, Judy could also be seen talking with the French or Australians, trying to wheedle a tidbit out of a syndicate spokesman or directing questions at the retreating back of one of the helmsmen as he tried to escape down the dock. One would see Judy with a pencil stuck in her long yellow-blond hair—muscular tanned legs below short, tight shorts and

"One would see Judy Lawson with a pencil stuck in her long yellow blonde hair . . ."

disarmingly innocent blue eyes searching out the innermost thoughts of her interviewee.

It is not surprising that Washington's Mutt and Jeff kept up a friendly rivalry that must have made interesting reading back home. In Newport, *The Star-News* came out on top if only because it was able to refrain from bolting for the press boat's rail while *The Post* could not. It was with triumphant glee that Duncan entered the press boat's saloon one rough day to announce, "*The Washington Post* is walking rapidly around the deck trying not to be seasick, but I think the effort will not succeed."

A few minutes later an only slightly subdued *Washington Post* announced that, indeed, the battle had been lost.

THE ULTIMATE FAN

It was just before the America's Cup series began in 1964 that *Yacht Racing*'s editor Bruce Kirby asked me, "Say, have you met the Canadian fellow who says 'fuck' all the time?" I laughed and told Bruce that I didn't think I had.

"I met him in 1962," Kirby explained. "He's a real America's Cup fanatic. He's been to every series, and I saw him again today. His name is Walker. Every other word he says is 'fuck,' and his pretty, blonde wife just smiles sweetly as if nothing strange had happened at all."

Thus even before I had met Walker, I'd gotten his name straight —he was "Jack Fucking Walker." Unlike today, when you can hear anything said in public, in 1964 when I met Jack and Diana Walker that word was heard only in the commoner Thames Street bars, and then only in rare outbursts. To hear it being said in a conversational tone while having dinner in the posh Canfield House, with a very attractive Diana Walker—mother of three—was disconcerting in the extreme.

Jack earned his middle name for good in 1967 with the unforgettable description of an *Intrepid* crew member, calling him "David Rocke———feller."

So infectious is Jack Walker's colorful speech that Pam Donovan, editor of a sailing annual, took Jack's expletives home with her and spread them among those in her office. The indiscriminate interjection of the particular verb concerned and its past participle may become an English-language epidemic in the name of its most frequent user.

One would be mistaken to assume that Jack is crass or crude. Quite the contrary. With the notable exception that a certain word is used frequently, Jack is a thoughtful, polite, well mannered, intelligent, interesting, witty graphic-designer and America's Cup nut supreme. His enthusiasm for everything to do with the America's Cup is pleasantly overwhelming.

Jack has always been an Australian fan. He met Alan Payne, *Gretel*'s 1967 challenger, and they too became good friends. Hood and his wife Julie spent a week at Jack's home in Montreal after the Cup series and presented Walker with Hood's Sydney Yacht Squadron necktie. In 1970 Walker met Jim Hardy, re-established his friendship with Payne, and in 1974 he met Hardy's brother, Tom.

Walker always manages to wangle himself a press pass. He attends all the press conferences, tags along whenever we can sneak him onto one of the 12-Meter docks, and soaks up the atmosphere like

Jack F. Walker, America's Cupophile Supreme!

a sponge that's spent a thousand years on the moon. After missing the first race because of the fog, he bought his way aboard the press boat, *Hel-Cat*, at twice the price of the excursion steamers. For Jack it was well worth it.

"I guess it begins as we drive into Newport," said Walker, describing his feelings about the America's Cup. "It's like coming down the last leg on a screaming reach with the spinnaker set and the whole fleet behind you (Walker's 24-footer usually leads the fleet on Montreal's Lake St. Louis). And then our wheels hit the old cobblestones of Thames Street, bump along past Christie's with the first stop at the Press Headquarters, where it all begins. We seek out the guys we know and haven't seen since the last Cup series, and somewhere in the crowd you find an American Ted Jones, a Canadian Bruce Kirby, an Australian Bob Ross, and over there, laughing like some kind of Coney Island laughing machine, is that crazy Englishman Bob Fucking Fisher. Then I know we've checked into Newport.

"Probably the highlight of this summer would be the night we tied up alongside Ted Turner's motor sailer and went aboard. You'll recall how Ted was upset about losing out on *Mariner* and to compensate for his rejection he was contemplating a 'round-the-world race in *Windward Passage* (if he could talk her owner, Mark Johnson, into the idea). He'd take *Passage* from Seattle down the West Coast to Panama and up to New York. Then a shakedown cruise to London, leave London for the start, slide down the coast, hang a left, watch out for icebergs . . . 'Nobody really cares. The energy crisis will eventually get us all anyway,' said Turner. On to Sydney, around the Horn, and a pleasant romp back to London.

"For me," Walker continued, "it was just incredible that anyone would even consider such an around-the-world adventure, and here was Turner talking about it as if he really was going to do it—which he probably will!

"I really enjoyed that evening immensely.

"The other nights in The Candy Store with reservations for four and five people turn up. The maitre d' is firm but polite. Then we repeat the performance a few nights later. The maitre d' is ready for the nut house!

"When we get to the races as seen from the press boat, *Hel-Cat*, we know the results five minutes after the start, but we come back for more. Like, anyone paying $120 a day to see two boats following each other around a 24-mile course has got to be missing a few screws! I figured each 'free' beer was costing me $30 and I had to drink a lot of beer at that.

"But the excitement is there just the same: the starting-line maneuvers, the spectator fleet, the little boats, big boats, fantastic yachts, and even the *Hel-Cat* is kind of fun. The people you meet aboard—old friends, new friends, all have that common interest.

"Ocean Drive: a lazy afternoon is spent watching the surf, Jonathan Livingston Seagull, and friends. Then it's back to the hotel for a shower and out to dinner and a few laughs. The Electric Elephant, acid rock, unrelated to 12-Meter yachts, but nevertheless we're there and we laugh and dance and go back to The Pearl for a late nightcap.

"We meet a crazy-bearded New Zealander and take him up to our room because he has no place to sleep. I think Diana picked him up but she says I did. 'Smoke marijuana?' he asks, and I say, 'Sure, I'll smoke anything,' expecting any minute to have the door kicked in and get thrown out of the hotel and into jail.

"In the morning I wake up with an incredible hard-on, and Diana says, 'but, Jack, there's that guy with the beard snoring in the other bed,' and by the time I get rid of him it's time to go down to the *Hel-Cat* again.

"That night it's Leo's Family Dining Room, a place to eat good food and a place to discuss little boats in twenty-foot waves, photography, clam chowder, steamed clams, and boiled lobster.

"Then the final party at the Australian's pad, meeting the Hardys, enjoying good wine. We all go down to The Candy Store for fun and games. It is a night, a summer, an America's Cup to remember.

"Leaving Newport is always sad, but never quite like this time. I hope there will be many more Newports for all of us. The day I miss an America's Cup it'll be because I'm six feet under."

Like many an Australophile, Walker was not too turned on by Alan Bond, and didn't root for *Southern Cross* with his usual abandon. For the first time since the resumption of the series in 1958, Walker realized that, were the challenger to win, it would mean the end of America's Cup series as he has come to know and love it. No America's Cup, no Newport, no "Jack Fucking Walker," the world would not be nearly so much fun!

"BONDMANSHIP"

On Monday, August 26, after it was announced that Dennis Conner would join the *Courageous* crew as starting helmsman, Alan Bond issued the following statement.

"We are extremely apprehensive and concerned to learn of Conner's appointment specifically in the role of starting helmsman.

"Conner has a reputation as an aggressive helmsman in Congressional Cup match racing, and we are fearful that fouling and striking tactics will be introduced to America's Cup starts.

"These tactics are an accepted part of Congressional Cup racing, but would prove extremely dangerous if used in actual America's Cup events. Conner has already been involved in three protest situations during the present U.S. elimination series, proving that his approach is one of pressure tactics along the lines of Congressional Cup racing, rather than on the codes of strict sailing skills of crew and boat.

"We deplore this approach, which is degrading to the dignity and prestige of the America's Cup as one of the world's most important sporting events. We are most concerned that this style of racing could be condoned by the New York Yacht Club, to seriously disadvantage our efforts.

"Apart from the unsportsmanlike nature of this approach, there is a definite element of danger to the safety of the crews and boats by adoption of rodeo tactics afloat."

Bond's attack on Dennis Conner was premature from two standpoints. The Aussies had yet to win against the French, and it was at least in questionably bad taste for Bond to infer that his yacht would be the challenger. Secondly, it was still to be decided if *Courageous* would be the defender. Thus Bond also insulted the *Intrepid* group. There are specific rules governing the start and other maneuvers. Unless those rules are infringed there is no cause for complaint. If a rule is broken, an official protest should be lodged. It is surely unsportsmanlike to protest a competitor in the press.

This type of gamesmanship is typical of Alan Bond. In engaging in it he stoops to the low levels of conduct he professes to defend. Naturally, neither the New York Yacht Club nor the *Courageous* Syndicate responded to Bond's statement, which he later denied was an "outburst" against the Americans. By such ploys as this Bond maintained a double standard whereby he demanded strict adherence to standards by others but refused to hold to those standards himself.

One wondered if Jim Hardy, who has always been the epitome of a gentleman, could continue to accept Bond's behavior. Would he not get branded by association as adhering to principles in which he did not believe? Could Hardy accept this, and if not, wouldn't it have an effect upon his performance as *Southern Cross*'s skipper? Indeed, wasn't the entire crew to appear the sort of ruffians that Bond appeared to be, and would they perform at their best under the circumstances?

There are many who would have wished the Aussies luck in their quest for the America's Cup, but few who wanted them to win as long as Bond was their spokesman and leader.

The general dissatisfaction with Alan Bond's conduct made him open to ridicule on other fronts. He had been accused of financing his challenge with Japanese money, which he denied, and all sorts of people were chortling over the fact that stock in Bond's development company had plummeted along with the general decline in the world economy.

Yanchep Sun City came in for its share of yuks. One English journalist who had been there called it "Ratshit Fly City."

"Until the sea breeze comes in to blow them into the desert," he said, "the flies cover the place. They are so big they knock aside the cork on a bushman's hat—there's a two-dollar bounty on the wings of the bloomin' things!"

Still others wondered aloud if Bond could be charged with misleading advertising by promoting Yanchep Sun City as the site of the 1977 America's Cup, if he lost the Cup.

One reporter wanted to ask Bond if the change in hailing port from "Yanchep Sun City" to "Fremantle" was changed, as was rumored, at the insistence of the Royal Perth Yacht Club because it violated the IYRU rule against advertising on a yacht. It was also rumored that Bond planned to change it back and make an issue of it with the New York Yacht Club in the America's Cup series. Of course, Bond never did change the hailing port from "Fremantle," which is the name of the port at Perth.

Bond made himself so thoroughly obnoxious to the press that many idle hours were spent thinking up ways to get him with impunity. One veteran reporter suggested something like this: "It would be unfair to characterize Alan Bond as a —————." (Each could insert his favorite invective.)

By far the best characterization of Bond that managed to get into print was written by Steve Cady of *The New York Times* following Bond's alleged outburst against Dennis Conner and *Southern Cross*'s defeat of *France*. Cady wrote, "Since launching his publicity-drenched challenge, Bond has put an 'absolute rubbish' label on the notion that the Cup might be primarily a sporting venture. Earlier this week, he accused the New York Yacht Club of degrading the dignity of the Cup by introducing 'dangerous rodeo tactics' to starting line maneuvers.

"Today, he stirred resentment among his own troops by proposing to put himself aboard *Southern Cross* for what turned out to be the completion of a 4–0 sweep over *France* in their series for the role of cup challenger. Bond sailed as far as the starting area as a member of the crew and then apparently changed his mind about competing in the race. He was transferred to a tender.

" 'The boys aren't too happy about it,' said an Australian journalist. 'I mean, they've been training two years and now Bondy puts himself onto the boat to handle one of the coffee-grinder winches. A good winch man is supposed to be able to lift his own weight.'"

Cady went on to say, "In the aristocratic eyes of the N.Y.Y.C., Bondy [sic] is simply the wrong kind of person to be challenging for a trophy as sacred as the America's Cup. His money is new, made on penny and dollar stocks and later on land speculation, and his manners are terrible. Brash when he arrived here, he is now being described as boorish and uncouth. Worst of all, he appears to have come up with an extremely fast 12-Meter.

"Unperturbed, Bond refuses to stop throwing brickbats and start yelling 'Hip, Hip Hurrah!' He is the basketball player falling over backward to draw a charging foul, the boxer complaining to the referee about below-the-belt punches, the baseball batter asking the umpire to inspect the ball to see whether the pitcher is throwing illegal spitters."

Actually, Bond could be very charming if the situation pleased him to be. He was like a chameleon changing its color to suit its surroundings, and one never knew quite how he would react to different situations. Nevertheless, one found oneself almost liking the man at times when he appeared charming, likable, and sincere. At such rare occasions one had to remind oneself that this was Alan Bond, whom you were supposed to dislike, and that it was unfashionable to have such nice thoughts about someone who was supposed to be a scoundrel. Friends who entertained the Australians at their home in Jamestown found Bond a very pleasant sort and wondered what all the fuss was about his reputed bad behavior.

Bond was not above contradicting himself without apologies if it suited his purpose to take an opposite stand from a previous position. An amusing example of this occurred after the final race between *France* and *Southern Cross*. Bond refused to sit under the battery of clocks, supplied by the Rolex Watch Company, showing the current time at the various cities throughout the world where people would be interested in America's Cup activities. When asked why he refused to sit under the sign, Bond replied that as far as he was concerned Rolex was not a sponsor of the America's Cup. Bruno Bich, Jean-Marie Le Guillou, and the entire assemblage had to wait about fifteen minutes while workmen removed the sign, before Bond would sit down and the press conference could begin. Bond either had not noticed the sign being there for the previous press conference or at least if he had, he

Alan Bond discourses after third race against *France*, apparently unaware of Rolex Watch sign behind him. The next press conference was delayed for fifteen minutes when Bond demanded the sign be removed before he would allow press conference to begin.

chose to ignore it. The flap apparently was caused because the Rolex Watch Company had given each crew member of each contender a free watch. Bond had wanted a watch for *Gretel II*'s crew as well as *Southern Cross*'s crew, and Frank Rohr of Rolex had balked.

On Tuesday, September 17, the following item appeared under the letterhead of the Southern Cross America's Cup Challenge Association Limited signed by R. C. Hemery, who was their press relations man:

MEDIA CORPS

Mr. Rene Dontan, President Rolex Watch U.S.A. Inc. will present Rolex Watches to all [roman added] *members of this team at 7* P.M. *tonight in the Australian team sail-loft.*

R. C. Hemery

It is not known whether Frank Rohr will attend!

LOG FROM ABOARD "HEL-CAT"— THE AMERICA'S CUP MATCH

An America's Cup is difficult to see. The course centers around a buoy 7 miles offshore. Spectator craft are held behind a cordon of patrol vessels 500 yards from the course. And that's the closest one gets. When the yachts sail to the port-tack lay line, the spectators 500 yards outside the starboard-tack lay line are lucky to see two white specks. At 500 yards you can't tell one Twelve from another when you're aboard a small boat bobbing in the wash of a thousand other vessels. From the deck of an excursion steamer you can make out some of the action through binoculars if it's not foggy. If you are one of a select eighty-odd accredited members of the press lucky enough to have a pass on one of the big 210-foot Coast Guard cutters, you get a pretty good view all the way around the course (provided there is no fog) although you can't make out any details as to who aboard may be steering or what sails the yachts are using.

13

In past years, most of the writers and all but a few photographers were confined to the large cutters, and a small group of hard-core sailing-magazine, daily-newspaper, and radio/television types were allowed aboard one of the inside patrol vessels. However, this 95-footer was subject to the call of the Flotilla Commander for patrol duty. Often it would be ordered away just when things got interesting.

It is obviously pointless (not to say dangerous) to try to see anything from one's own boat, so, for the America's Cup match itself, *Gamecock*'s role was reduced to that of floating hotel in Newport Harbor, which left the problem: how to witness and photograph the event.

For this match, and for the first time in recent Cup history, the press had its own "private" viewing platform. Ralph Ianuzzi, who handles publicity for the New York Yacht Club, arranged the charter of the party fishing boat *Hel-Cat II*, a 65-foot steel catamaran, which normally operates out of Montauk, Long Island. *Hel-Cat* was available for fourteen days and, best of all, Ianuzzi had arranged with the N.Y.Y.C. for *Hel-Cat* to have "privileged vessel" status—one of the eighteen official vessels allowed inside the patrol area. With her bright red hull, yellow superstructure, plain pipe railings, rusty anchor swinging from one of her twin bowsprits, and her polyglot crew of reporters and photographers, *Hel-Cat* cut a jaunty and incongruous slash through the polished yachts and uniformed crews of the New York Yacht Club brass.

Hel-Cat was uncomfortable, wet, crowded, and inglorious, "like a half-tide rock in a breeze of wind," reported Duncan Spencer in *Soundings*, but she was the nearest thing to heaven to those of us lucky enough to be aboard. Besides the view, there was brandy for the morning coffee, all the beer one could consume, and the camaraderie of one's fellow nautical scribes from Washington, Sydney, London, New York, Cowes, and Peoria all for an elegant fee.

We were not to be disappointed in *Hel-Cat*'s advantages although the first day some of us feared we would be banished from our privileged status forever. We cringed when in lining up for the parade through the spectator fleet to the starting line, George Glas, *Hel-Cat*'s unflappable captain, bellowed through his bull horn at the Chairman of the America's Cup Committee. Captain Glas decided the yacht was out of position and let it be known decisively. We positively shuddered with embarrassment when *Courageous* and *Southern Cross* headed

The America's Cup Buoy plastered
with stickers saying, "Beat the
Blunder from Down Under."

straight for *Hel-Cat,* which had drifted out of position, in their pre-start maneuvers, elated at having the view and yet fearful that *Hel-Cat*'s transgression would certainly result in the loss of our inside view. We did not realize at that point that both 12-Meter skippers planned to use this group of inside spectators regularly to try to wipe off the other's cover.

Hel-Cat was indeed a privileged spot, and in the fog, nearly the only spot from which to see the action.

Aboard Hel-Cat: *Tuesday, September 10*
Weather: Fog. Wind SSW 11 knots.

After winding around Hel-Cat *at the 10-minute gun, so close we can see the fillings in Dennis Conner's molars,* Courageous *holds* Southern Cross *up until both yachts are over the starting line. Cross tacks away just before the starting gun.* Courageous *bears away and they start on opposite tacks. It is about even with* Courageous *maybe having a slight lead.*

This is the most exciting part of the series. Competitors, spectators, syndicate investors, yacht designers, and yacht-club officials find out at this point whether the summer has been a worthwhile effort or a futile blunder. The yachts come together for the first time in that desperate, yet painfully slow, lunge for the first windward mark. The yacht that attains it first most likely will win the series, but it may take many minutes before there is a sign of which yacht is faster.

Courageous *is on starboard at the leeward end of the line and* Southern Cross *is on port.* Courageous *tacks to cover and appears to have a slight edge. As both yachts go out toward the port-tack lay line they appear to be . . . No, it's impossible to tell which one might be ahead. First one appears to lead, then the other. It's extremely close!*

Southern Cross *tacks and we're about to find out whether the America's Cup is safe or if we're going to Australia. As they come together,* Courageous *on port tack, giving right-of-way to* Cross,

Hundreds of spectator craft churn Rhode Island Sound into a sea of confusion. The Coast Guard always manages somehow to keep the curious spectator captains from seriously interfering with the competitors.

doesn't appear to be able to cross the Aussies. *She can't. Instead she tacks underneath* Southern Cross *and ahead and in the "safe leeward" position. It looks like* Cross *is on top, but* Courageous *has her wind free. This is one helluva boat race!*

Hood works Courageous *up underneath* Cross, *but it is a painfully slow process.*

In these conditions, gains are measured in inches and minutes rather than feet and seconds or miles and hours. It is an agonizing process, and even if it plays out with one yacht gaining the advantage over the other, the tactical situation can reverse their roles. The situation approximately three-quarters of the way up the first weather leg was this.

In the fog it was impossible to see the mark. The yachts were very near the lay line—perhaps able to fetch the mark without tacking. With *Courageous* ahead and to leeward she would be ahead if they fetched the mark, but if neither could make it on this tack or if *Cross* could fetch but *Courageous* couldn't, then *Southern Cross* would surely round first. If neither could fetch, *Cross* could most likely prevent *Courageous* tacking for the mark until both were well past. Being able to tack first, *Southern Cross* would have the advantage.

For the first time in recent America's Cup history, the competitors used the spectators as a tactical weapon. As *Courageous* and *Southern Cross* came together for the first time, the press boat *Hel-Cat* found herself in the middle of the pre-start maneuvering.

Slowly, inexorably Hood works Courageous *up underneath. It is an act of will as if he is picking her up and moving her bodily sideways—like moving a knight on a chess board, two squares ahead and one square over. From 200 yards away we can feel the concentration of the skippers as Hood thinks, "Up, up, catch that wave just so and up another inch." Hardy is at a disadvantage not knowing*

*how much to foot off for speed or how much to point up to keep out
of* Courageous's *backwind. Bit by bit the tension eases as* Courageous
*works up and ahead to lie directly in front of her rival. After half
an hour, the defender has an advantage of 100 feet in distance and
a few seconds in time.*

Courageous bears away and Cross *is in her wake. They have
overstood the windward mark and now Hardy is forced to sail the
last quarter-mile in Hood's backwind.*

Courageous moved away to lead by 5 boatlengths at the mark.
That was the race. Barring some fluke or miscalculation, *Southern
Cross* would not be able to get past. Even with superior speed on the
reaches and the run—which did not materialize—the Australian
yacht would have little chance to win.

Courageous bore away from
Southern Cross and put *Hel-Cat*
between herself and her rival
thereby keeping the Aussies from
getting on the Defender's stern.

*As the yachts jibe for the second reaching leg, I am standing
with Australian newsman Piers Akerman.*
"Well, it's all over," says Piers.
"What do you think is the problem?"
"Slow boat," he says with resignation.

above. Conner at the helm and Hood just forward of him duck as *Courageous*'s boom crosses over her deck as she jibes.

opposite above. Aboard *Hel-Cat* we could practically reach out and touch *Courageous* as she came sweeping past.

opposite below. Conner and Hood ignore the shouts of astonishment and encouragement from the press corps and concentrate on the task at hand—controlling *Southern Cross.*

The tactic works, and *Courageous* comes out of her 360° turn in a controlling position, too leeward and slightly astern of *Southern Cross*.

"Bad tactics," says another Aussie. "Hardy should have tacked before they reached the lay line, then maybe he would have had a chance."

The rest of the race was anticlimactic. In a fading wind and visibility so limited that the spectators saw virtually nothing, *Courageous* moved steadily ahead to finish with a final margin of nearly ¾ of a mile and 5 minutes.

Fog delayed the start, and the yachts did not finish until 1830. By the time they came into the harbor it was dark, but crowds lined the piers along the harbor. As she moved to her lift at Newport Shipyard's north yard alongside her tender, *Courageous*'s short journey was like a racing-car's victory lap. Bathed in the dim light from the city, amid shouts, cheers, horns, whistles, and applause, Ted Hood waved in acknowledgment and then he and his crew disappeared into the night.

Aboard Gamecock: *Wednesday, September 11*
Weather: Foggy and calm.

The fleet is waiting in the harbor this morning until the Race Committee's yacht, Carltina, *signals that they are proceeding to the race course. Waiting for the fog to lift, we read in* The New York Times, *". . . The America's Cup is safe—quite safe." Prophetic, perhaps, but I don't believe it yet. Had* Southern Cross *been able to scratch out a few yards on the first weather leg yesterday, the outcome might have been completely reversed.*

Carltina has just radioed that there will be no race today. We will have to wait until tomorrow before we know how safe the America's Cup really is.

Someone asked Jim Hardy if he had any trouble sleeping after his first race defeat. "Aw no," said Hardy. "I slept like a baby—woke up every two hours and cried."

Aboard Hel-Cat II: *Thursday, September 12*
Weather: Hazy, visibility reported to be a mile and a half at Block Island, improving to two miles occasionally. Wind SW 10 knots.

Conditions don't look too good as we pass the Castle Hill, but there is enough visibility to go out to the rendezvous point.

On the America's Cup course it is quite foggy. Visibility appears to be about a mile. Course signals go up as scheduled at noon.

Just before the 10-minute gun *Courageous* and *Southern Cross* began tentative maneuvers approaching each other to jockey for position. Once again both yachts headed toward the fleet of privileged spectators clustered outside the America's Cup buoy at the port extension of the starting line. It appeared one of them was going to try a wipe-off maneuver similar to the one used by *Courageous* on Tuesday. (In anticipation of a repeat of Tuesday's maneuvers, the Flotilla Commander had cautioned all privileged vessels to hold position and not try to get out of the way should the yachts sail into their midst.)

Both yachts were on starboard tack. They split on either side of one of the large yachts, and *Cross* tacked onto port. *Courageous* did not tack—as perhaps Hardy had anticipated she would—and *Cross* could not clear her bow. *Courageous*, with the right-of-way, held her course, forcing the Australian to tack hurriedly. They were very close, and it was at least questionable if *Southern Cross* could complete her tack in time to avoid fouling *Courageous*. *Cross* did not appear to complete her tack, but held high, forcing *Courageous* to luff to avoid a collision. Here was a clear case of an infringement of the racing rules.

The rules that apply in this case are the following:

36—FUNDAMENTAL RULE

A PORT-TACK *yacht* [Southern Cross] *shall keep clear of a* STARBOARD-TACK *yacht* [Courageous].

41—TACKING OR JIBING

1. *A yacht which is either* TACKING *or* JIBING [Southern Cross] *shall keep clear of a yacht* ON A TACK [Courageous].

2. *A yacht shall neither* TACK *nor* JIBE [Southern Cross] *into a position which will give her right of way unless she does so far enough from a yacht* ON A TACK [Courageous] *to enable this yacht to keep clear without having to begin to alter her course until after the* TACK *or* JIBE *has been completed.*

3. *A yacht which* TACKS *or* JIBES [Southern Cross] *has the onus of satisfying the Race Committee that she completed her* TACK *or* JIBE *in accordance with rule 41.2.*

Courageous headed up, slowly filled away on the port tack, and immediately flew a protest flag. *Southern Cross* held head to wind for a few seconds and tied a protest flag to her backstay.

Later at the protest hearing, the International Jury disallowed both protests, saying that it was "satisfied that *Southern Cross* complied with the obligations laid upon her by rule 41" and that, "*Southern Cross* did not establish to the satisfaction of the International Jury that *Courageous* bore away from her close-hauled course...."

The accompanying photographs clearly show that *Courageous* was fouled. The incident occurred within clear view of the International Jury but on the opposite side from which these photographs were taken. It is possible that the Jury's view was not as clear as it would have been there and that *Courageous*'s prosecution of her case was inept. *Southern Cross*'s protest was a trumped-up affair, and it is entirely possible that the whole situation was orchestrated by Alan Bond (he was aboard *Cross*) to create an incident. If *Southern Cross* was not bent on some nefarious scheme, then its maneuvers were simply inept boat handling of the type one hopes not to see among novices at the local boat-club level but occasionally does. Surely such ineptitude is not expected on the America's Cup course. On the other hand, if *Southern Cross* was deliberately put in position to foul *Courageous*, then the Australians were stooping to the low level of comportment that Bond earlier accused Dennis Conner of espousing.

At the start of the second race with *Courageous* and *Southern Cross* once again sailing among the eighteen yachts that comprised the privileged spectator fleet containing officials, press, and photographers. Perhaps thinking that Dennis Conner would try to wipe *Southern Cross* off on the vessel flying flag #12, *Southern Cross* tacked onto port.

opposite above. As they passed either side of yacht #12 (hidden behind *Southern Cross*), it became apparent that the yachts would pass very close to each other at least, and most likely, were on collision course. *Southern Cross*, being on starboard tack, had the right-of-way.

opposite below. As the Twelves converged it was quite clear that *Southern Cross* could not clear *Courageous*. In fact, if they had continued *Courageous* would have hit her just abaft amidships.

above. Holding on until too late, *Southern Cross* tacked just under *Courageous*'s bow.

opposite above.   The point of foul. Note that *Courageous* appears to have headed up to avoid collision as indicated by the backwinding of her mainsail (the slight hollow between the "US" and "26" of her sail insignia.)

opposite below.   Inches apart, the two yachts almost head to wind. Note that the top of *Courageous*'s genoa is backed with the leech pressing against the upper spreader. This is a clear indication that the foul did occur, as she alleged.

above.   *Courageous* tacked away onto port following the foul, which occurred virtually under the nose of the judges' boat, which is the trawler yacht just to leeward of *Courageous* in the right of the picture. The America's Cup buoy is to the left. There were protests from both yachts. However, the jury disallowed both protests, saying that a foul had not occurred. With the advantage of hindsight and a photographic record of the incident, it would appear that the jury erred in its decision. However, the

decision had no effect on the outcome of the race or the series, as *Courageous* won the race in any event.

Of course, it didn't matter whether the Jury disqualified *Southern Cross* or not—she lost the race. By denying Bond the out that a disqualification would have provided him, the Jury avoided criticism and public ridicule by Bond. Nevertheless, it is at least one opinion that a blatant foul occurred, that *Southern Cross* should have been disqualified in the interests of fair sailing even though it meant no difference in the score.

Both yachts start even on port tack, having been wary of each other following the [alleged] foul, Courageous *tacks away onto starboard and* Southern Cross *tacks to cover.* Courageous, *ahead and to leeward, sucks up underneath* Cross *in much the same way that she did in the critical minutes of the first race.*

Once again, *Courageous* proved superior to windward and *Southern Cross* was forced to tack away. *Courageous* tacked to cover, and it appeared that a long, dismal afternoon parade would ensue. *Southern Cross* tacked away, and *Courageous* cleared her bow easily.

Already the Aussies and other Australian fans aboard Hel-Cat *are muttering about Bond, Hardy, slow boat, bad tactics, and lumping them altogether into one catch-all phrase, "the blunder from down under." One sums it up with the question, "Didja expect to see anything else?"*

Many of us have gone into Hel-Cat's *cabin for lunch when there is a mighty shout from the bow. Rushing on deck, we see that* Southern Cross *has crossed* Courageous! Cross *is ahead, but inexplicably, she continues for a full 2 minutes before tacking to cover* Courageous.

They had been too close for *Southern Cross* to tack directly on *Courageous*'s wind, but it did not seem reasonable for *Cross* to sail so far on starboard tack before covering. If a wind shift had favored *Southern Cross* from her position ahead and to leeward on the port tack, a similar shift (or header) could subsequently favor *Courageous*, now to leeward on port tack. It made little sense for *Cross* to go off on her own as she did, and she violated the cardinal rule of match racing by not putting a close cover on her rival once she was ahead.

Courageous got away. When they came together on opposite tacks, *Courageous* passed ahead of *Southern Cross* by several boatlengths, and she stayed ahead. At the windward mark *Courageous* led by 34 seconds—exactly the same margin as in the first race.

Southern Cross appears to catch up on the reaches, but in fact she has not closed any distance. She is 28 seconds behind at the reaching mark and back to 34 seconds at the America's Cup buoy. They are still very close!

On the second weather leg they go into the classic tack-split, tack-split ballet that has become so familiar over the summer. Courageous *has not been able to cover precisely although* Cross *has not been sailed as aggressively as she might have been. Bob Ross of Australia's* Modern Boating *feels that the Australians are not as sharp as they might be. He doesn't think Jim Hardy is steering the boat as well as he should.* Cross *seems to continue to make tactical errors.*

Courageous *leads by 56 seconds at the fourth mark.*

The primary reason Hardy had not been more aggressive—initiating a tacking duel when behind going to windward—is that they had discovered early that *Courageous* was quicker "in stays" (tacking) than *Cross*. Every tack would cost the Australians half a boatlength or more. *Courageous* had superior acceleration and it was self-defeating for the Aussies to try to catch up by initiating a tacking duel.

The run is relatively uneventful. Courageous *maintains her lead with an official time at the downwind mark of 45 seconds. It is quite close really, and it would be interesting to see what would happen if* Southern Cross *could get to a windward mark in the lead. Could* Courageous *catch up? I doubt that she could. But the Aussies just don't seem to be able to sail as well tactically as* Courageous, *and that appears to be the difference.*

The wind picked up to about 15 knots for the final windward leg and *Courageous* finished ahead with a margin of 1 minute, 11 seconds. On the way into harbor one observer was heard to say, "It looks like there's going to be some soul searching by Mr. Bond tonight." And his companion replied, "No soul searching, mate—no soul!"

Aboard Hel-Cat: *Friday, September 13*
Weather: Clear. Wind SW at 10 knots forecast to increase to 20
knots by midafternoon.

Last night Southern Cross *was hauled out of water and work was done on her rudder. It appeared that she was not tracking as straight as* Courageous, *which knifes through the water in an absolutely dead straight line.*

Alan Bond sailed aboard Cross *yesterday, and two of her crew reported to Bob Fisher that Bond couldn't hack it on the grinder. It took guys from other jobs to spell Bond on the winch—so all is not happiness in the* Southern Cross *camp. However, today with the wind up to 15 or 16 knots and promising more we may very well see something different.*

Fifteen minutes before the start, the fog rolled in and we couldn't see *Carltina* from *Hel-Cat* at the opposite end of the starting line. Visibility continued to deteriorate as the fog blew into the area in great billowing clouds borne by the wind. At 10 minutes to go, we lost sight of the America's Cup buoy—visibility down to 150 yards—and at noon the *Carltina* signaled a postponement.

The fog lifted for about 15 minutes but it socked in again at 1325. The race was called off for the day at 1400.

It's significant that today we had the breeze that Southern Cross *was supposedly designed for—a good solid 18 to 20 knots with a good rough sea. It's too bad we were unable to get a race off as the weather pattern indicates that we may not get another day like this. The fog may become an important factor in this series.*

Aboard Hel-Cat: *Saturday, September 14*
Weather: Clear. A weak front has come through during the night and the haze and fog have finally blown away. Wind NW 12 knots.

The sea is quite chopped up from the spectator fleet and there are some leftover rollers from the sou'wester that blew for several days in advance of the front. The yachts will have a nasty, confused sea to contend with at the start.

Southern Cross gets the start, and scattered applause breaks out aboard Hel-Cat. *She is 8 seconds ahead of* Courageous *and right on top of her.* Southern Cross *drives down to gain speed, but* Courageous *continues to hold high—just slightly ahead and with clear wind. Both yachts appear to be even, but if I were asked to pick one, it would be* Courageous; *she appears to bounce less in the fading breeze—which is lightening all the time.*

Once again, Courageous *does her thing—coming up underneath* Southern Cross. *Five minutes after the start,* Courageous *is giving* Cross *a dose of backwind, and the Australian yacht is forced to tack away.*

The wind continued to fade as the leg progressed, and the yachts slowed to a crawl. Under these conditions, either yacht could get a private puff of wind and move ahead. Both yachts were sailing on port tack toward the lay line when *Southern Cross* sailed into a gigantic header.

"Tack! Tack!, you idiot, tack!" the Southern Cross *partisans cry from* Hel-Cat. *It's so loud that I'm sure Jim Hardy can hear it. If he does, he ignores the shouted advice and continues to sail into the header while it appears that he could easily cross* Courageous *on the other tack.* Cross *finally tacks, but it is on a lift that puts her behind* Courageous *once again, and a mighty groan shudders through the 70-odd chests aboard* Hel-Cat.

From that point the wind remained light, and it soon became apparent that they would not finish the course before the time limit expired. There was no stopping the race, however, and the dismal drama—with *Courageous* a mile ahead—ground to a futile conclusion at 1740 when time ran out.

On *Hel-Cat* the long day was spent in a series of dialogues cataloging the woes of *Southern Cross.* Speaking of Bond's futile effort Dr. Norris Hoyt said, "But he keeps trying. Like a monkey trying to write Shakespeare on a typewriter, he [Bond] keeps punching the keys."

Broadcasting to listeners in Australia, Lou d'Alpuget, in a brilliant three-minute monologue, explained it this way:

. . . What Bond likes to call his wonder boat continues to perform like a blunder boat. I'm convinced it's not an inherent fault in the design of the yacht, but the way skipper, Jim Hardy, and his crew handle her in critical occasions. Once again today Hardy made a truly brilliant start, outsmarting the American starting helmsman, Dennis Conner, in Courageous *during the preparatory period before the gun and cleverly holding him stalled below the line for more than a minute. . . . Conner had earlier twice attempted to sweep in under the lee quarter of* Southern Cross *in order to force her over the line but Hardy skipped clear, climbed neatly to windward and held the defender below him. Twenty seconds before the gun Hardy eased* Southern Cross *just half a length high and continued to pin* Courageous *below him. If Conner had cleared away immediately and gone for the line he might have made it with a safe leeward berth, but he waited, perhaps 10 seconds too long, while the Australian boat, two lengths to windward and footing fast, shot through with the eight seconds to spare that she gained at the start. The breeze was then 10 knots from the northwest and the boats made good pace as they set out on their first windward beat. If it had been that breeze all the way and had held in strength and direction* Southern Cross *might have performed a great deal better. But the nor'wester here in Rhode Island is a land breeze and an especially fickle one. As it faded, the Australian effort started to fall apart. First,* Courageous *inexorably squeezed up from leeward and desperately* Southern *Cross's sheet tailers, especially when she was on starboard tack, began to flatten on their gear to try to get their windward position.*

It slowed down the boat in the lightening air and ultimately they had to tack to avoid the turbulence coming out of Courageous's sails. After three tacks it was still lightening and variable breeze, Southern Cross was only a length behind and still well within striking distance. But then, after 16 minutes of sailing, the Australians seemed to lose their heads completely. They kept overtrimming the headsail on the starboard tack and they sailed off to the northward on a temporary 20-degree windshift while their shrewd rivals kept working to the westward of the lay line anticipating a truly big windshift from the southwest. And when it came Courageous established a truly colossal advantage of 300 yards in a matter of minutes and a margin of three minutes when they rounded the first mark. That turned the 3.8 mile reach into a work, and the next leg, which was to have been a port spinnaker reach, into a starboard one. Southern Cross gained nothing in distance but in the steadier winds, for a period, was only 1 minute, 17 seconds behind at the windward mark and one-thirty odd when they turned for the second beat for which officials moved the rounding mark 105 degrees. And on the second beat Courageous just poured it on until the southwesterly breeze died, too. And then the time limit ran out. And so the score remains Courageous—2, fog—2, clock—1, Southern Cross—zero."

There was no race on Sunday, September 15 and *Southern Cross* was again hauled out and her articulated rudder was replaced with the more conventional rudder she had used most of the summer.

Aboard Hel-Cat: *Monday, September 16*
Weather: Clear. Wind W 8 knots, forecast to become SW.

Both yachts sail away far from the line toward the Coast Guard's square-rigged barque, Eagle, which is anchored at one corner of the patrol area, 500 yards to leeward of the America's Cup buoy. They gradually work their way back toward the starting line with about 8 minutes to go.

With 2 minutes to go, Courageous gets underneath Southern Cross, and both yachts go head to wind. At a minute and a half to go, both fall off, gather way, and they go for the line.

Dennis Conner put both yachts over the line early. It was a close call, but the recall numbers were displayed for both yachts. (The Aussies claimed *Courageous*'s "26" was displayed a long time before *Southern Cross*'s "4." Bondsmanship again?)

Courageous came back first, jibing around for the line. Being to windward, *Southern Cross* had to take the slower route and tack before bearing away for the line. *Courageous* easily won the restart and sailed away in commanding position.

Courageous maintained a very tight cover on *Cross* going up the first windward leg, covering her tack for tack. They appeared to get to the starboard side lay line very early—in fact, *Courageous* failed to cover *Cross* at one point, thinking they could both fetch the mark, but a slight current kept pushing both yachts to the southeastward, forcing them to take several more tacks before rounding. *Courageous* led by 45 seconds at the first mark, and poured it on thereafter to finish the race 3 minutes, 32 seconds ahead of *Cross*.

After the finish, Alan Bond and Jim Hardy were overheard talking over the radio to discuss whether they should agree to race the next day or to call for a lay day.

Bond, sarcastically: "I don't know why you'd want to race tomorrow."

Hardy, plaintively: "We tried, Alan, we really tried."

Bond: "Just trying for a little humor, Jim. We might as well race tomorrow."

Aboard Hel-Cat: *Tuesday, September 17*
Weather: Clear. Wind SW 12 knots.

Again the yachts sail down toward Eagle. *At the 5-minute gun they are both on port with* Courageous *to leeward and ahead, and they take a slow zigzag course, first lifting and then falling off as they sail over toward the Committee Boat. At 3 minutes to go they sail head to wind.*

With 30 seconds left, both yachts are on port tack with very little way. Cross *tacks for the line, and* Courageous *tacks around her. This is incredible!* Courageous *has just leaped ahead. One second she was even with* Cross *with both yachts moving very slowly and now she is flying out in front going for the line. It's fantastic! At the start* Courageous *has a 20-second lead.*

There was very little to the race after the excellent start by *Courageous* except to see how far behind *Southern Cross* could get. Although the wind for the last race was well below that which *Southern Cross* was supposed to like, it was the strongest and steadiest wind of the series. *Courageous* opened up her lead at every mark. Especially to windward, she simply ran away from the Australian yacht.

It was a crushing defeat. *Southern Cross* finished 7 minutes, 19 seconds behind the defender.

The start of the last race showed *Courageous*'s vastly superior acceleration. Both yachts were headed away from the line with a little over a minute to go to the starting gun. Being close aboard and to leeward, *Courageous* had to wait for *Southern Cross* to tack first.

Southern Cross tacked for the line, and Conner immediately followed.

During her tack, *Courageous* sailed right around her rival to complete the maneuver in a commanding position to windward . . .

. . . the most decisive starting triumph of the series.

Three cheers for a worthy opponent
from the victorious *Courageous*
crew.

The long, sad return to port for the
loser accompanied by a troupe of
loyal supporters and curious
onlookers all sailing on a sea
glittering in the late afternoon
sunlight.

Shore-bound spectators lined
several deep along the sea wall at
Fort Adams to share in the merri-
ment of the returning flotilla.
Southern Cross leads *Courageous*
whose mast can be seen over the
head of the spectator sitting on the
wall. Hans Isbrandtsen is just
visible as he performed an
impromptu high-wire act on
Courageous's upper spreaders.

opposite left. Other spectators await the successful defender aboard a dinghy in *Courageous*'s slip—complete with a glass of bubbly in celebration.

opposite below. Hood, Conner, and two other crew members are joined in the traditional victor's dunking by syndicate head Bob McCullough (in straw hat) and crew boss Sam Wakeman. Even-tually, nearly everyone in sight took a swim including Olin Stephens, *Courageous* designer, and, unex-pectedly, Race Committee Chair-man William Foulk.

opposite right. Also unexpectedly, the couple in the dinghy got dunked as well, and the girl—no longer with the bubbly—received a helping hand strategically placed!

below. There was little to be joyful about aboard the unsuccessful chal-lenger as the crew received condol-ences from wives, sweethearts, and friends and drank the last of Alan Bond's America's Cup beer. Jim Hardy (center) talks with Aus-tralian journalists.

above. The Aussies joined the *Courageous*'s crew celebration, swapping shirts with their rivals. Bob McCullough dons a white sweater from a *Southern Cross* crewman.

below. Seemingly all of Newport jams aboard *Courageous* threatening to sink her while the overflow crowd threatens to capsize her tender *Escort*.

opposite above. At the final press conference Alan Bond congratulates the winning skipper, Ted Hood, while Bob McCullough looks on.

opposite below. Later at press conference, Bond tells of his disappointment at losing so decisively. From left to right the principals from each yacht are: Ted Hood, *Courageous*'s skipper; Olin Stephens, *Courageous*'s designer; Bob McCullough, *Courageous* Syndicate Manager; Victor Romagna, moderator; Bond; Jim Hardy, *Southern Cross*'s skipper partially obscured by Bob Miller, *Southern Cross*'s designer.

HINDSIGHT

What went wrong? How could the match that had been touted so
highly turn into such a runaway? Where did the *Southern Cross*
group make mistakes? Is there any hope that a challenger can ever
overcome the will of the New York Yacht Club's members to defend
the Cup at all costs?

14

With the advantage of hindsight, it is clear that two major
factors caused *Southern Cross*'s downfall: inexperience and lack of
preparedness.

It is true that Alan Bond gathered some experienced people
around him. In Jim Hardy, John Bertrand, and Dick Sargent he had
crew members who had raced previously in America's Cup competition. However, Bond ignored much talent in Australia, which, if
brought to bear on his challenge, could have helped immeasurably
in avoiding pitfalls of the past. The choice of designer was particu-

larly unfortunate. While Bob Miller has had considerable experience with offshore racing yachts and has been one of the best small-boat sailors in Australia, he had no previous experience in the very specialized field of 12-Meter design. That *Southern Cross* was as good as she is speaks well for Miller's talent and ingenuity, but he was led astray by tank data and intuitive ideas that perhaps would have been avoided by a more experienced man. Had Bond had the services of Alan Payne, designer of *Gretel II*, which some think was the fastest 12-Meter in the world (and still may be), things might have been quite different.

Quoted in *Sail* in an article titled "What Went Wrong," Jim Hardy said, "Everything about Alan Payne's concept in *Gretel II* was right. For instance, he appreciated the problem of the chop from the spectator fleet and the need for windward performance, especially the advantage of being able to come out of tacks fast. . . ." Hardy should know—he skippered both yachts in America's Cup competition.

Bond's team lacked preparedness, which showed in the tactical errors *Southern Cross* made in the final series. They were small, dumb mistakes that showed a lack of sharpness rather than a lack of knowledge or experience. *Southern Cross*'s crew simply hadn't put their skill on the line against a tough competitor. Their four races against *France* were not taxing. They could have blown her off easily, they knew it, and they did. The *Southern Cross* crew members were soft from not having to exercise the muscles between their ears.

The *Southern Cross* group also evidenced their unpreparedness in several ways. They never did settle down on one rudder—continuing to switch back and forth between more or less conventional shapes and the Italian made articulated rudder. The latter gave better control, but made it difficult for Hardy to obtain any "feel" of the yacht.

"When I turned the wheel of *Southern Cross*," Hardy was quoted in *Sail* as saying, "I felt every mechanical part move and the whole system was too elastic."

The rigging was completely changed aboard *Southern Cross* between the series with *France* and the America's Cup match. Bruce Stannard, the most fiercely loyal of all the Australian reporters, took great pride in showing me the very thin rods that were being installed for *Cross*'s new standing rigging. I thought it was terribly late to be making major changes. Even though the rigging was impressively small and would undoubtedly reduce weight and windage aloft, and I assumed the engineering had been worked out, I would have been fearful that some unforeseen difficulty could result in failure and, perhaps, dismasting. It wouldn't have been quite so bad if they'd had a spare of the mast they were using, but it was the only one of its kind—the spares were completely different.

In the same article in *Sail*, Jim Hardy said, ". . . I wasn't in favor of changing, but Bob Miller was firm. But I think that the light rigging was so elastic that we must have been giving away some windward ability."

If you have twelve hours on the clock in which to prepare for a race, by the time the little hand gets to nine the fiddling should stop and you should go sailing. At this point the little hand was relatively past eleven, and the Aussies were still fiddling.

A continuing series between *Southern Cross* and *Gretel II* could have made a tremendous difference. Suppose Bond had kept John Cuneo as skipper of *Southern Cross* and Jim Hardy as skipper of *Gretel II* and told them after they arrived in Newport to have at each other. "Here's a million dollars each, boys, do anything you want with it, and the winner will meet *France* for the right to challenge for the America's Cup."

There is certainly the possibility that *Gretel II* is just as fast as *Southern Cross*, and in the conditions encountered in the America's Cup series, probably faster. When both yachts were sailing together early in the summer, *Gretel* was faster in many conditions, but they gradually got *Southern Cross* up to speed so that she could beat *Gretel* almost all the time. However, Jim Hardy's comments to Bruce Kirby— proving *Southern Cross* faster by slowing *Gretel II* down—became very telling. It was a serious error because *Gretel II* legally could have been the challenger and, perhaps, should have been.

Had Bond allowed this sort of competition, had he realized the value of a hard-fought series such as the N.Y.Y.C. syndicates always have, had he allowed *Gretel II* to be a contender instead of simply a trial horse, things might have turned out differently. *Southern Cross* still might have been the challenger, but she would have won that right by hard work rather than been given it by decision of the director, who, as it turned out, lacked the experience to make a correct decision on this important point.

There was yet another factor that had a subtle effect on the defense. At the final press conference after *Courageous* won the fourth race, her syndicate manager, Bob McCullough, said to Bond, "You frightened us so badly, Alan, that we worked that much harder to defend the Cup."

It was quite true that Bond had pumped out so much advance publicity on how tough his yacht was going to be and how determined he was to win the Cup that very few people failed to take him seriously. A little bit of planned bungling early would have gone a long way to ease the pressure on the New York Yacht Club. In fact, with less urgency in the defense, *Courageous* might not have been built. How difficult it would have been to raise the money if people had regarded the Australian effort with the same casualness they showed toward the French once Elvström was out and the new French yacht cancelled. Imagine how differently things might have been if *Intrepid* had only *Mariner* and *Valiant* to push her. Suppose that *Intrepid's* backers had thought it not worth the bother—let the new *Mariner* Syndicate handle it. The Cup would be in Australia now.

Surely the message is clear that there *is* a formula for winning the America's Cup. Follow the lessons of the defenders, and gradually hone a good machine—yacht, sails, and crew—to perfection, as Olin Stephens has been able to do with his 12-Meter designs and as Ted Hood and others have been able to do with sails. Weld a strong crew together with the heat of competition and, if possible, make the whole thing look casual and amateurish. Then, and only then, a challenger will have an even chance to win the America's Cup.

The French may be able to do this although their flirtation with Paul Elvström may have distracted from their own continuity. Elvström himself could put this type of effort behind a challenge, but he has yet to get into the competition and gain actual experience. The Australians have had the best opportunities to build, but each of their syndicate heads has had an ego problem and refused to be associated in any way with past failures. The Aussies have a bad habit of shunning everything that has been associated with a failure. They throw out the baby with the bath water. If their next effort could include the experience of Jim Hardy, John Cuneo, Dick Sargent, Hugh Treharne, Peter Cole, Alan Payne and, if possible, the recent experience of Bob Miller, they might be able to pull it off. But they won't, or will they?

Jack Walker would like to mount a Canadian challenge, but he admits that he probably never could raise enough money. We were talking about it one evening toward the end of the series and Jack expounded his theories on the ideal way to run a challenge. He recounted his discussion with Tom Hardy, brother of *Southern Cross*'s skipper, about the possibility of a Hardy Brothers' challenge, which Tom told him would be "low key."

"When we do our Canadian challenge," said Walker, "it will be *super* low key. We're going to lull them into complacency. Our boat's going to need a coat of paint, our sails will look old and stained. Instead of sharp uniforms for the crew, each will wear faded cut-off jeans and old plaid shirts with solid patches. They'll grow scruffy beards and need haircuts. They'll fight and bicker among themselves in public. They will lie around and smoke pot all day instead of working on the boat, and they'll get drunk every night and chase wild women. Everyone will think we're a pushover and no one will work hard to beat us. When the series begins we'll be sharp and skillful, and we'll win the fucking America's Cup four straight!"

"What you need," I suggested, "is eleven sets of twins. The bad twins appear in public, while the good twins practice in secret and get sharp."

"There you go," said Walker. He thought a minute and then added, "I know two sets of twins in Montreal, good sailors, too."

"Yeah," said Diana, "but they're all girls."

Tara Ann Nicholson, *Courageous*
fan through thick and thin.

NEWPORT REVISITED

Two weeks after the America's Cup, Tara Ann Nicholson, her sister Maura, and her friend Dawn Whiston drove down to Newport from Wheaton College. Tara wanted to have a last look around at her adopted summer home. She wanted to show Maura and Dawn some of the things she had done and some of the places she had grown to love.

15

They went first to the Black Pearl. Tara's outdoor cafe had been transformed back to its original function—a parking lot. Inside, old friends turned to say, "Hi," then turned away, absorbed in something new in which Tara had not shared. Next door, at The Candy Store, there wasn't a soul she knew.

Never mind, go down to Newport Shipyard to the pier where *Courageous* had docked. There she was, but her mast was out. No one was around, and *Courageous* looked so forlorn—like a once favorite but now forgotten toy. Tara had to admit, things were pretty grim, and she began to wonder why she had come back.

"Oh well, let's drive out to Hammersmith Farm," she thought. Maura had never been there the brief times she had visited Newport earlier, and Tara had neglected to take a photograph of the beautiful estate that had played such an important role in her summer. This was where the *Courageous* crew had lived, and Tara had spent many hours here commiserating over *Courageous*'s defeats and reveling in her triumphs.

Swinging her car confidently around the bend just before reaching Hammersmith's long and stately driveway, Tara prepared a smiling greeting for the guard she knew would recognize her, expecting his friendly wave as she zipped between the stone gates. Instead, Tara was greeted by iron bars and a "No Trespassing" sign. Everyone had gone. Hammersmith Farm had been closed and shuttered for the winter.

Tara kicked herself for being such an idiot. She never should have come, that was now obvious. With a sagging heart she headed for Castle Hill, her favorite spot two miles down the road. There was her friends the Walshes' hotel where the French had stayed. Near the hotel is the little stone lighthouse that guards the entrance to Narragansett Bay and the beautiful meadows above rock outcroppings which tumble down to the sea.

Gone were the handsome Frenchmen. In their place, two white haired ladies rocked in the afternoon sun, wrapped in knitted shawls against the chilly autumn breeze. Maura and Dawn ran through the fields to explore the cliffs and watch the seagulls dropping clams onto the rocks below.

Sitting in her car, Tara leaned against the steering wheel, pressed her eyes into the crook of her elbow, and cried.

APPENDIX:
REPORT OF THE RACE COMMITTEE

New York Yacht Club
PRELIMINARY TRIAL RACES

Sailed off Newport, Rhode Island under the observation of The America's Cup Committee

MONDAY, JUNE 24, 1974   **FIRST RACE**

Start at C. Course: A–F. Distance: 13.5 miles.
Wind: At start 75°, 8 knots. At finish 87°, 18–20 knots.

	Division I			**Division II**		
	Courageous	Intrepid		Mariner	Valiant	
Official Start	12:30			12:35		
1st Mark	13:15:50	13:15:31	00:19	13:27:41	13:29:55	02:14
2nd Mark	13:47:44	13:47:53	00:09	13:57:27	13:59:14	01:47
Finish	14:07:28	14:07:41	00:13	14:17:35	14:19:28	01:53

SECOND RACE

Start at D. Course: A–H. Distance: 13.5 miles.
Wind: At start 90°, 14 knots. At finish 85°, 18 knots.

	Intrepid		Mariner	
Official Start		15:25		
1st Mark	16:12:54		16:14:14	01:20
2nd Mark	16:42:44		16:45:29	02:45
Finish	17:02:29		17:05:21	02:52

TUESDAY, JUNE 25, 1974

Racing cancelled due to high winds and high seas.

WEDNESDAY, JUNE 26, 1974   **THIRD RACE**

Start at C. Course: Z–B–C–Z (Course shortened at Mark Z). Distance: 21.7 miles.
Wind: At start 30°, 15 knots. At finish 40°, 8 knots.

	Division I			**Division II**		
	Intrepid	*Valiant*		*Courageous*	*Mariner*	
Official Start	12:20			12:35		
1st Mark	13:19:25	13:21:52	02:27	13:39:42	13:41:54	02:12
2nd Mark	13:41:46	13:44:21	02:35	14:02:21	14:04:41	02:20
3rd Mark	14:20:16	14:24:19	04:03	14:42:24	14:46:26	04:02
Finish	15:28:34	15:38:54	10:20	15:51:14	16:01:00	09:46

THURSDAY, JUNE 27, 1974　　　　　　　　　　**FOURTH RACE**

Start at C. Course: A–E (Course shortened to finish at Mark E). Distance: 10.5 miles.
Wind: At start 75°, 6 knots. At finish 180°, 4 knots.

	Division I			**Division II**		
	Courageous	*Intrepid*		*Mariner*	*Valiant*	
Official Start	12:15			12:30		
1st Mark	13:28:06	13:30:53	02:47	13:34:08	13:35:56	01:48
Finish	14:11:46	14:13:43	01:57	14:19:04	14:20:52	01:48

FIFTH RACE

Start at Z. Course: E–B. Distance: 11.5 miles.
Wind: At start 220°, 4 knots. At abandonment 210°, 2 knots.

	Division I		**Division II**	
	Intrepid	*Mariner*	*Courageous*	*Valiant*
Official Start	16:25		16:40	
Race Abandoned	17:51:50		17:51:50	

FRIDAY, JUNE 28, 1974　　　　　　　　　　**SIXTH RACE**

Start at E. Course: B–H–E–B. Course shortened at Mark E. Distance: 10.5 miles.
Wind: At start 090°, 15 knots. At finish 085°, 24 knots.

	Division I			**Division II**		
	Intrepid	*Mariner*		*Courageous*	*Valiant*	
Official Start	12:15			12:30		
1st Mark	12:51:56	12:54:14	2:18	13:07:55	13:10:11	2:16
2nd Mark	13:14:22	13:17:37	3:15	13:30:32	13:33:26	2:54
Finish	13:29:47	13:32:35	2:48	13:45:30	13:48:44	3:14

SATURDAY, JUNE 29, 1974　　　　　　　　　　**SEVENTH RACE**

Start at Z. Course: D–B–Z–D. Distance: 22.1 miles.
Wind: At start 220°, 12 knots. At finish 235°, 16 knots.

	Intrepid	*Courageous*	
Official Start		11:30	
1st Mark	12:16:09	12:17:34	01:25
2nd Mark	12:44:04	12:45:35	01:31

	Intrepid	*Courageous*	
3rd Mark	13:05:20	13:06:04	00:44
4th Mark	13:48:11	13:49:26	01:15
Finish	14:20:48	14:22:10	01:22

EIGHTH RACE

Start at Z. Course: G–Z–G. Distance: 11.1 miles.
Wind: At start 235°, 15–16 knots. At finish 235°, 17 knots.

	Intrepid	*Courageous*	
Official Start		15:30	
1st Mark	15:59:25	15:59:48	00:23
2nd Mark	16:18:15	16:18:41	00:26
3rd Mark	16:45:22	16:48:09	02:47
Finish	17:04:24	17:07:34	03:10

New York Yacht Club
OBSERVATION TRIAL RACES
Sailed off Newport, Rhode Island under the observation of The America's Cup Committee

SATURDAY, JULY 13, 1974　　　　　　　　　　**FIRST RACE**

Start at Z. Course D–U. Distance: 12.5 miles.
Wind: At start 215°, 5 knots. At finish 220°, 8 knots.

	Courageous	*Intrepid*	
Official Start		11:20:00	
Actual Start	11:20:49	11:20:37	00:12
1st Mark	12:37:25	12:36:42	00:43
2nd Mark	13:16:41	13:17:03	00:22
Finish	13:40:03	13:40:59	00:56

SECOND RACE

Start at Z. Course: F–Z–G–Z–G shortened at G. Distance: 15.2 miles.

	Courageous	*Intrepid*	
Official Start		14:40:00	
Actual Start	14:40:08	14:40:05	00:03
1st Mark	15:16:58	15:16:08	00:50
2nd Mark	15:44:33	15:44:19	00:14
3rd Mark	16:12:07	16:11:23	00:44
4th Mark	16:33:54	16:33:27	00:27
Finish	17:01:57	17:01:09	00:48

SUNDAY, JULY 14, 1974　　　　　　　　　　**THIRD RACE**

Start at U. Course: W–V–U–W. (Bearing to W 215° M) Shortened at U. Distance: 10.5 miles.

Wind: At start 215°, 4 knots. At finish 210°, 5 knots.

	Courageous	Valiant	
Official Start		12:05:00	
Actual Start	12:06:45	12:05:07	01:38
1st Mark	13:29:55	13:27:58	01:57
2nd Mark	13:57:02	13:56:36	00:26
Finish	14:37:07	14:38:19	01:12

FOURTH RACE

Start at U. Course: W–U–W. (Bearing to W 205° M) Shortened at U. Distance: 9 miles.
Wind: At start 205°, 7 knots. At finish 210°, 6 knots.

	Courageous	Valiant	
Official Start		15:35:00	
Actual Start	15:35:10	15:35:16	00:06
1st Mark	16:22:02	16:24:11	02:09
Finish	17:07:59	17:10:42	02:43

MONDAY, JULY 15, 1974   FIFTH RACE

Start at U. Course: D–X–U–D. (Bearing to X 215° M) Distance: 18.6 miles.
Wind: At start 255°, 14 knots. At finish 245°, 16 knots.

	Valiant	Intrepid	
Official Start		11:55:00	
Actual Start	11:55:01½	11:55:02	00:00½
1st Mark	12:30:28	12:29:38	00:50
2nd Mark	12:47:18	12:46:09	01:09
3rd Mark	13:06:10	13:04:41	01:29
4th Mark	13:43:32	13:40:45	03:47
Finish	14:12:51	14:09:49	03:02

SIXTH RACE

Start at U. Course C. Distance: 10.4 miles.
Wind: At start 245°, 16 knots. At finish 240°, 8 knots.

	Valiant	Intrepid	
Official Start		15:05:00	
Actual Start	15:05:10	15:05:09	00:01
1st Mark	15:55:51	15:53:42	02:09
Finish	16:36:47	16:34:55	01:52

TUESDAY, JULY 16, 1974   SEVENTH RACE

Start at H. Course: U–Z–H–U. Shortened at H. Distance: 9.7 miles.
Wind: At start 120°, 6.5 knots. At finish 165°, 5 knots.

	Intrepid	Courageous	
Official Start		13:05:00	
Actual Start	13:05:06	13:05:08	00:02
1st Mark	14:14:10	14:14:50	00:40
2nd Mark	14:59:53	15:00:15	00:22
Finish	15:17:51	15:19:15	01:24

WEDNESDAY, JULY 17, 1974   EIGHTH RACE

Start at D. Course: W–C–D–W. Shortened at W. Distance: 13.9 miles.
Wind: At start 225°, 8 knots. At finish 225°, 6½ knots.

	Courageous	Valiant	
Official Start		14:05:00	
Actual Start	14:05:08	14:05:08½	00:0½
1st Mark	14:54:21	14:57:29	03:08
2nd Mark	15:26:05	15:29:51	03:46
3rd Mark	15:41:00	15:44:50	03:50
Finish	16:48:01	16:49:05	01:04

THURSDAY, JULY 18, 1974   NINTH RACE

Start at T. Course: W–V–T–1st Repeater. Distance: 18.7 miles.
Wind: At start 225°, 11 knots. At finish 215°, 15 knots.

	Intrepid	Valiant	
Official Start		11:55:00	
Actual Start	11:55:03	11:55:05	00:02
1st Mark	12:35:43	12:37:05	01:22
2nd Mark	12:53:32	12:55:19	01:47
3rd Mark	13:14:12	13:16:20	02:08
4th Mark	13:54:54	13:57:50	02:56
Finish	14:24:11	14:27:27	03:16

TENTH RACE

Start at T. Course: X–T–1st Repeater. Distance: 12 miles.
Wind: At start 215°, 18 knots. At finish 220°, 18 knots.

	Intrepid	Valiant	
Official Start		15:20:00	
Actual Start	15:20:03	15:20:01	00:02
1st Mark	15:48:53	15:49:09	00:16
2nd Mark	16:09:27	16:09:43	00:16
3rd Mark	16:44:34	16:44:28	00:06
Finish	17:05:38	17:05:10	00:28

SATURDAY, JULY 20, 1974   ELEVENTH RACE

Start at C. Course: G–C–G. (Bearing to G 025° M) Shortened at C; Distance: 8 miles.
Wind: At start 025°, 3–5 knots. At finish 225°, 5 knots.

	Courageous	Intrepid	
Official Start		13:05:00	
Actual Start	13:05:04	13:05:23	00:19
1st Mark	14:06:37	14:07:56	01:19
Finish	15:11:14	15:15:46	04:32

TWELFTH RACE

Start at C. Course: W–A–C–W. (Bearing to W 225° M)
Wind: At start 225°, 6 knots.

	Courageous	Intrepid	
Official Start		16:00:00	
Actual Start	16:00:53	16:00:48	00:05

Race abandoned on first leg at 16:46:40 due to lack of wind.

SUNDAY, JULY 21, 1974   THIRTEENTH RACE

Start at Z. Course: W–Z–D, Shortened at Z. Bearing to W 200° M, Distance: 9 miles.
Wind: At start 200°, 6 knots. At finish 215°, 10 knots.

	Courageous	Valiant	
Official Start		12:35:00	
Actual Start	12:35:04	12:35:16	00:12
1st Mark	13:20:06	13:22:58	02:52
Finish	14:07:31	14:11:11	03:40

FOURTEENTH RACE

Start at Z. Course: D–X–Z–D. Bearing to D 215° magnetic.
Course shortened at Z: Distance: 10.8 miles.
Wind: At start 215°, 11 knots. At finish 245°, 11 knots.

	Courageous	Valiant	
Official Start		14:55:00	
Actual Start	14:55:23	14:55:42	00:19
1st Mark	15:47:40	15:51:43	04:03
2nd Mark	16:12:17	16:16:37	04:20
Finish	16:30:21	16:35:17	04:56

MONDAY, JULY 22, 1974   FIFTEENTH RACE

Start at America's Cup Buoy. Course: America's Cup. Distance: 24.3 miles.
Bearings: 1st Leg 195°, 4th Leg 195°, 6th Leg 205°.
Wind: At start 190°, 6 knots. At finish 205°, 8 knots.

	Intrepid	Courageous	
Official Start		12:10:00	
Actual Start	12:10:05½	12:10:06	00:00½
1st Mark	12:59:28	13:00:20	00:52
2nd Mark	13:22:41	13:23:23	00:42
3rd Mark	13:44:59	13:45:28	00:29
4th Mark	14:29:27	14:30:38	01:11
5th Mark	15:12:48	15:13:09	00:21
Finish	15:59:14	16:00:14	01:00

TUESDAY, JULY 23, 1974   SIXTEENTH RACE

Start at America's Cup Buoy. Course: America's Cup. Distance: 24.3 miles.
Bearings: 1st, 4th and 6th legs 155°.
Wind: At start 155°, 12 knots. At finish 160°, 10 knots.

	Intrepid	Courageous	
Official Start		12:15:00	
Actual Start	12:15:04	12:15:03	00:01

	Intrepid	Courageous	
1st Mark	13:02:39	13:03:17	00:38
2nd Mark	13:25:20	13:25:46	00:26
3rd Mark	13:46:44	13:47:04	00:20
4th Mark	14:33:47	14:35:07	01:20
5th Mark	15:12:14	15:14:27	02:13
Finish	16:01:45	16:03:43	01:58

WEDNESDAY, JULY 24, 1974   SEVENTEENTH RACE

Start at H. Course: U–Z–H–U. Shortened at Z. Distance: 7.6 miles.
Wind: At start 130°, 6 knots. At finish 185°, 6 knots.

	Intrepid	Valiant	
Official Start		11:50:00	
Actual Start	11:50:09	11:50:14	00:05
1st Mark	12:33:36	12:36:25	02:49
Finish	13:10:44	13:13:38	02:54

EIGHTEENTH RACE

Start at Z. Course: X–Z–X. (Bearing to X: 195° M) Shortened at X. Distance: 9 miles.
Wind: At start 195°, 6 knots. At finish 195°, 6 knots.

	Intrepid	Valiant	
Official Start		13:55:00	
Actual Start	13:55:14	13:55:18	00:04
1st Mark	14:36:09	14:37:16	01:07
2nd Mark	15:18:19	15:19:06	00:47
Finish	15:56:06	16:04:03	07:57

New York Yacht Club
FINAL TRIAL RACES 1974

THURSDAY, AUGUST 15, 1974   FIRST RACE

Course: America's Cup Course. Distance: 24.3 miles.
Wind: At start 202°–225°, 9 knots. At finish 210°, 11 knots.

	Division I			Division II		
	Intrepid	Courageous		Mariner	Valiant	
Official Start	13:45			14:00		
Actual Start	13:45:02	13:45:12	00:10	14:00:49	14:01:08	00:19
1st Mark	14:33:02	14:33:39	00:37	14:43:22	14:44:49	01:27
2nd Mark	15:00:02	15:01:33	01:31	15:12:23	15:14:12	01:44
3rd Mark	15:22:08	15:23:16	01:08	15:34:59	15:36:09	01:10
4th Mark	16:08:32	16:08:17	00:15	16:23:43	16:25:19	01:36
5th Mark	16:47:24	16:47:16	00:08	17:03:37	17:06:55	03:18
Finish	17:34:36	17:35:07	00:31	17:51:32	17:53:04	01:32

FRIDAY, AUGUST 16, 1974　　　　　　　　　　**SECOND RACE**

Course: America's Cup Course shortened at fifth mark. Distance: 19.8 miles.
Wind: At start 185°, 6 knots. At finish 210°, 15 knots.

	Division I			Division II		
	Intrepid	*Courageous*		*Courageous*	*Valiant*	
Official Start		12:25			12:40	
Actual Start	12:25:57	12:25:11	00:46	12:40:46	12:40:47	00:01
1st Mark	13:30:30	13:29:41	00:49	13:35:41	13:38:15	02:34
2nd Mark	13:57:47	13:58:02	00:15	14:02:58	14:07:08	04:10
3rd Mark	14:20:40	14:21:17	00:37	14:26:11	14:30:14	04:03
4th Mark	15:04:48	15:06:22	01:34	15:10:37	15:15:10	04:33
Finish	15:37:43	15:39:10	01:27	15:42:49	15:48:21	05:32

THIRD RACE

Course: Windward-Leeward starting at America's Cup buoy. Distance: 9 miles.
Wind: At start 210°, 15 knots. At finish 220°, 14 knots.

	Division I			Division II		
	Intrepid	*Valiant*		*Courageous*	*Mariner*	
Official Start		16:30			16:45	
Actual Start	16:30:12	16:30:27	00:15	16:45:19	16:45:17	00:02
1st Mark	17:13:17	17:14:50	01:33	17:30:34	17:33:04	02:30
Finish	17:45:34	17:48:18	02:44	18:04:06	18:06:54	02:48

NOTE:　Race No. 2—Intrepid protesting Mariner and Mariner protesting Intrepid
　　　　Race No. 3—Mariner protesting Courageous

SATURDAY, AUGUST 17, 1974　　　　　　　　**FOURTH RACE**

Course: America's Cup Course. Course changed at fourth mark to 190°. Distance: 24.3 miles.
Wind: At start 205°, 15 knots. At finish 190°, 15 knots.

	Division I			Division II		
	Courageous	*Intrepid*		*Mariner*	*Valiant*	
Official Start		12:25			12:40	
Actual Start	12:25:10	12:25:09	00:01	12:40:05	12:40:07	00:02
1st Mark	13:07:59	13:07:41	00:18	13:22:04	13:21:39	00:25
2nd Mark	13:29:26	13:29:02	00:24	13:43:59	13:43:27	00:32
3rd Mark	13:51:42	13:51:21	00:21	14:06:58	14:06:29	00:29
4th Mark	14:34:18	14:33:35	00:43	14:39:16	14:39:36	00:20
5th Mark	15:10:52	15:10:40	00:12	15:25:16	15:25:56	00:40
Finish	15:51:19	15:51:21	00:02	16:08:40	16:09:26	00:46

MONDAY, AUGUST 19, 1974　　　　　　　　　**FIFTH RACE**

Course: America's Cup Course. Bearing to first mark 200°. Bearing to second mark changed to 230°. Course shortened at fifth mark. Distance: 19.8 miles.
Wind: At start 190°, 6 knots. At finish 230°, 5 knots.

	Division I			Division II		
	Intrepid	*Mariner**		*Courageous*	*Valiant*	
Official Start		14:45			15:00	
Actual Start	14:46:02	14:45:07	00:55*	15:00:06	15:00:46	00:40
1st Mark	15:33:28	15:32:58	00:30*	15:48:30	15:51:49	03:19
2nd Mark	16:10:56	16:10:34	00:22*	16:24:24	16:27:56	03:32
3rd Mark	16:34:31	16:34:22	00:09*	16:47:49	16:51:29	03:40
4th Mark	17:25:17	17:27:53	02:36	17:37:15	17:44:16	07:01
Finish	18:17:07	18:19:46	02:39	18:31:22	18:38:10	06:48

TUESDAY, AUGUST 20, 1974　　　　　　　　　**SIXTH RACE**

Course: America's Cup Course. Bearing to first mark 125°. Bearing to fourth mark changed to 160°. Course shortened at 5th mark. Distance: 19.8 miles.
Wind: At start 110°, 10 knots. At finish 180°, 7 knots.

	Division I			Division II		
	Intrepid	*Valiant**		*Courageous*	*Mariner**	
Official Start		12:40			12:55	
Actual Start	12:40:16	12:40:13	00:03*	12:55:10½	12:55:10	00:00½*
1st Mark	13:26:44	13:30:15	03:31	13:41:28	13:44:06	02:40
2nd Mark	13:59:17	14:05:18	06:01	14:14:59	14:18:28	03:29
3rd Mark	14:23:27	14:29:39	06:12	14:37:55	14:41:34	03:39
4th Mark	15:09:28	15:18:46	09:18	15:22:50	15:29:26	06:36
Finish	15:51:54	16:02:04	10:10	16:03:31	16:11:41	08:10

Following this race the America's Cup Committee excused Mariner and Valiant.

WEDNESDAY, AUGUST 21, 1974　　　　　　　**SEVENTH RACE**

Course: America's Cup Course. Bearing to first mark 100°. Bearing to fourth mark changed to 140°. Course shortened at fifth mark. Distance: 19.8 miles.
Wind: At start 90°, 5 knots. At finish 155°, 6 knots.

	Courageous	*Intrepid**	
Official Start		12:40	
Actual Start	12:40:20	12:40:04	00:16*
1st Mark	13:38:34	13:41:41	03:07
2nd Mark	14:27:05	14:30:02	02:57
3rd Mark	14:55:38	14:58:29	02:51
4th Mark	16:00:24	16:03:09	02:45
Finish	17:11:18	17:12:49	01:31

FRIDAY, AUGUST 23, 1974　　　　　　　　　**EIGHTH RACE**

Course: America's Cup Course. Bearing to first mark 165°. Course shortened at third mark. Distance: 10.86 miles.
Wind: At start 165°, 6 knots. At finish 130°, 8 knots.

	Courageous	*Intrepid*	
Official Start		13:00	
Actual Start	13:01:20	13:01:46	00:26
1st Mark	14:06:16	14:11:27	05:11
2nd Mark	14:28:34	14:33:51	05:19
Finish	15:00:20	15:05:11	04:51

NINTH RACE

Course: Windward–Leeward with start at America's Cup Buoy. Course to mark 220°, 4.5 miles. Distance: 9 miles.
Wind: At start 280°, 15 knots. At abandonment 340°, 10 knots.

	Courageous		Intrepid	
Official Start		16:35		
Actual Start	16:35:04		16:35:52	00:48
1st Mark	17:08:23		17:09:36	01:13

Race abandoned at 17:15:00.
INTREPID was recalled at start.

SATURDAY, AUGUST 24, 1974 — TENTH RACE

Course: America's Cup Course. Bearing to first mark 245°. Bearing to fourth mark changed to 235°. Distance: 24.3 miles.
Wind: At start 245°, 11 knots. At abandonment 235°, 10 knots.

	Courageous		Intrepid	
Official Start		11:50		
Actual Start	11:50:11		11:50:13	00:02
1st Mark	12:33:55		12:34:05	00:10
2nd Mark	12:55:07		12:55:16	00:09
3rd Mark	13:21:42		13:22:02	00:20

Race abandoned at 14:07:00 because of poor visibility.

SUNDAY, AUGUST 25, 1974 — ELEVENTH RACE

Course: America's Cup Course. Bearing to first mark 205°. Bearing to fourth mark changed to 230°. Bearing to sixth mark changed to 240°. Distance: 24.3 miles.
Wind: At start 198°, 10 knots. At finish 100°, 8 knots.

	Courageous		Intrepid	
Official Start		15:10		
Actual Start	15:11:22		15:11:54	00:32
1st Mark	16:03:26		16:03:43	00:17
2nd Mark	16:32:17		16:32:30	00:13
3rd Mark	16:53:31		16:53:41	00:10
4th Mark	17:48:51		17:49:38	00:47
5th Mark	18:42:24½		18:42:41	00:16½
Finish	19:41:55		19:42:05	00:10

COURAGEOUS being protested by INTREPID

TUESDAY, AUGUST 27, 1974 — TWELFTH RACE

Course: America's Cup Course. Bearing to first mark 195°. Bearing to sixth mark changed to 205°. Distance: 24.3 miles.
Wind: At start 195°, 15 knots. At finish 210°, 17 knots.

	Intrepid		Courageous	
Official Start		11:50		
Actual Start	11:50:07		11:50:09	00:02
1st Mark	12:33:25		12:33:09½	00:09½

	Intrepid	Courageous	
2nd Mark	12:54:01	12:54:16	00:15
3rd Mark	13:14:35	13:14:53	00:18
4th Mark	13:57:48	13:58:28	00:40
5th Mark	14:30:52	14:31:25	00:33
Finish	15:16:05	15:17:17	01:12

WEDNESDAY, AUGUST 28, 1974 — THIRTEENTH RACE

Course: America's Cup Course. Bearing to first mark 225°. Distance: 24.3 miles.
Wind: At start 225°, 15 knots. At finish 225°, 15 knots.

	Intrepid		Courageous	
Official Start		11:50		
Actual Start	11:51:40		11:51:55	00:15
1st Mark	12:34:37		12:34:58	00:21
2nd Mark	12:54:23		12:54:44	00:21
3rd Mark	13:14:05		13:14:24	00:19
4th Mark	13:59:10		13:59:41	00:31
5th Mark	14:31:41		14:32:19	00:38
Finish	15:18:10		15:19:02	00:52

THURSDAY, AUGUST 29, 1974 — FOURTEENTH RACE

Course: America's Cup Course. Bearing to first mark 060°. Bearing to fourth mark changed to 050°. Bearing to sixth mark changed to 030°. Distance: 24.3 miles.
Wind: At start 060°, 10–12 knots. At finish 025°, 10 knots.

	Intrepid		Courageous*	
Official Start		13:50		
Actual Start	13:51:34		13:51:10	00:24*
1st Mark	14:43:46		14:44:47	01:01
2nd Mark	15:07:27		15:08:26	00:59
3rd Mark	15:49:45		15:51:47	02:02
4th Mark	16:56:53		16:58:19	01:26
5th Mark	17:37:56		17:39:44	01:48
Finish	18:33:11		18:34:05	00:54

FRIDAY, AUGUST 30, 1974 — FIFTEENTH RACE

Course: America's Cup Course. Bearing to first mark 225°. Distance: 24.3 miles.
Wind: At start 230°, 8 knots. At abandonment 220°, 5 knots.

	Intrepid		Courageous*	
Official Start		14:15		
Actual Start	14:15:53		14:15:18	00:35*
1st Mark	15:13:41		15:12:51	00:50*
2nd Mark	15:40:19		15:41:25	01:06
3rd Mark	16:18:23		16:18:55	00:32

Race abandoned at 16:37:00 because of approaching squalls.

SATURDAY, AUGUST 31, 1974

Race postponed at 13:45:00 for lack of wind.

SUNDAY, SEPTEMBER 1, 1974

Race postponed at 14:15:00 for lack of wind.

MONDAY, SEPTEMBER 2, 1974   **SIXTEENTH RACE**

Course: America's Cup Course. Bearing to first mark 040°. Bearing to fourth mark changed to 025°. Distance: 24.3 miles.
Wind: At start 040°, 18 knots. At finish 029°, 20 knots.

	Courageous		*Intrepid**	
Official Start		11:50		
Actual Start	11:50:50		11:50:43	00:07*
1st Mark	12:31:06		12:31:52	00:46
2nd Mark	12:44:40		12:45:36	00:54
3rd Mark	13:07:40		13:08:19	00:39
4th Mark	13:50:58		13:51:41	00:43
5th Mark	14:15:22		14:16:22	01:00
Finish	14:55:03		14:56:50	01:47

Sailing Instructions for
THE AMERICA'S CUP 1974

1. CONDITIONS

The Races will be sailed under the "Conditions Governing the Races for the America's Cup Nineteen Seventy Four", as amended, under the challenge of the Royal Thames Yacht Club dated December 18, 1970 for a Match in the International Twelve Metre Class.

2. CAPTAINS' MEETING

The Captains' Meeting will be held aboard the Race Committee Vessel CARLTINA at 2:00 p.m., September 9, 1974.

3. COURSES

Races shall start at the America's Cup Buoy anchored seven nautical miles S.S.E. (Magnetic) from Brenton Reef Light and shall be approximately 24³⁄₁₀ nautical miles in length.

Races shall consist of six legs. The first leg, to be approximately 4½ nautical miles in length, shall be from the starting buoy to a mark to windward; the second leg shall be from the first mark to a mark equidistant from the starting buoy and the first mark at a point on the circumference of a circle the diameter of which is the first leg; the third leg shall be from the second mark back to the starting buoy; the fourth leg shall be from the starting buoy to the first mark; the fifth leg shall be from the first mark to the starting buoy; and the sixth leg shall be from the starting buoy to the first mark, at which the finish line shall be established.

The various rounds of the course will resemble the diagram on Page 5 of the Conditions.

Marks are to be left on the same hand as the starting mark (America's Cup Buoy).

The Magnetic course of the first leg shall be signalled, and the mark vessel shall be started not less than 10 minutes prior to the warning signal.

In the event of wind shifts after a race has started, the Race Committee may move the weather mark for the fourth leg and/or the sixth leg of the Course. The new magnetic bearing of the fourth mark and/or the Finishing Mark from the America's Cup Buoy will be signalled by the Committee Vessel or Auxiliary Committee Vessel which will be moving on a course from the America's Cup Buoy in a direction towards the yachts as they approach the America's Cup Buoy. In addition, this vessel will make a series of short sound signals as each yacht approaches.

Should the bearing of the fourth mark and/or Finishing Mark be more than 45 degrees to port or 135 degrees to starboard of the bearing of the previous windward mark, a special mark will be placed approximately 100 yards from the America's Cup Buoy. Yachts will pass between this special mark and the America's Cup Buoy, leaving the latter buoy on the proper hand and the special mark on the opposite hand.

Magnetic bearings will be signalled by three numeral penants from an after hoist of the Committee Vessel or Auxiliary Committee Vessel.

4. MARKS

The marks except the starting mark, which shall also serve as the third and the fifth marks, will be bright orange-red inflatable buoys cylindrical in shape. In the event a mark is missing an Auxiliary Committee Vessel will anchor in its place and display Code Flag MIKE and sound the International Morse Code M at intervals.

5. STARTING LINE

The Starting Line will be between a yellow flag on the Committee Vessel and the America's Cup Buoy.

6. FINISHING LINE

The Finishing Line will be between a yellow flag on the Committee Vessel and the first mark. Should the Committee Vessel be unable to move up to the Finish Line, an Auxiliary Committee Vessel shall take her place. This auxiliary vessel will then display a blue race committee flag in place of the yellow auxiliary race committee flag.

When in position at the Finish Line, the Vessel will display a Blue Cylinder until the time limit expires. In fog she will ring a bell rapidly, at intervals, for approximately five seconds. After sunset she will display the NYYC night signal (Green, Red, Green vertically) in place of the NYYC burgee.

7. STARTING PROCEDURES AND SIGNALS

1150	Course Signals	
1200	Warning Signal	One Yellow Cylinder
1205	Preparatory Signal	One Blue Cylinder
1210	Starting Signal	One Red Cylinder

Each cylinder shall be lowered thirty seconds before the hoisting of the next. Attention may be drawn to the making of each signal by the firing of a gun. The time of the starting signal shall be taken as the time of start of both yachts.

Yachts will be *racing* from the time of the Warning Signal.

8. RECALLS AND GENERAL RECALLS

Recalls shall be made in accordance with I.Y.R.U. Rules 8.1, 8.2(a), 8.3(a) and 8.3(b) which is modified to read: "Except as provided in Rule 31.2, Disqualification, rule infringements before the Warning Signal for the new start shall be disregarded for the purpose of starting in the race to be started."

The Committee Vessel will sound one blast on a horn for each yacht starting prematurely and will display block letters indicating which yacht started prematurely. The letters are black on white placards. They will be displayed at the starting line side of the Committee Boat. The letters will be removed from view as soon as the recalled yacht or yachts have wholly returned to the right side of the starting line or its extensions.

Letters KA	The Challenger
Letters US	The Defender

In the event of a general recall I.Y.R.U. Rule 51.1(c) shall *not* apply.

9. SPECIAL SIGNALS

Special Signals, including signals for postponements and abandonment, shall be made in accordance with I.Y.R.U. Rules 4.1 and 4.7.

10. TENDERS AND SUPPORT BOATS

Yachts shall release their tow and cast off from their support boats prior to the Warning Signal and in sufficient time to be at least 200 yards from them at the Warning Signal.

While racing competitors support boats shall not approach within 200 yards of either of the competing yachts, except as permitted by I.Y.R.U. Rule 59.

11. WILLINGNESS TO START ON THE NEXT DAY

After the leading contestant has finished or after the time limit has expired or after a race has been postponed or abandoned, the Race Committee will display Code Signal AQ inquiring the contestants' willingness to start the next day. Contestants must signal either Code Flag C (affirmative) or Code Flag N (negative) within one hour. The Committee will not haul down their signal until both contestants have replied and their signals have been understood.

12. PROTESTS

Protests shall be made in accordance with I.Y.R.U. Rule 68 and delivered to the Committee Vessel not later than three hours after the finish of the race concerned.

Protests will be heard by the International Jury aboard the committee Vessel.

RACE COMMITTEE

William H. Foulk, Jr., Chairman	Charles C. Adams, III
J. Henry Scholtz, Jr., Secretary	Robert B. Conner
E. Wesley Oliver, Jr.	C. Gaither Scott

AUXILIARY RACE COMMITTEE

B. Devereux Barker, III, James A. Carroll, Jr., Peter Geddes, Prescott W. N. Gustafson, George M. Isdale, Jr., Donald B. King, Charles F. Morgan, Nicholas Schaus, Frederick H. Scholtz, John B. Sinclair, Robert F. Walmsley, Jr., John M. Wright

MEASUREMENT COMMITTEE

James McGruer, Robert S. Blumenstock, A. E. Watts

INTERNATIONAL JURY

Dr. Beppe Croce, Chairman, Arthur R. Barron, Hon. Livius A. Sherwood

New York Yacht Club
AMERICA'S CUP RACES 1974

TUESDAY, SEPTEMBER 10, 1974   **FIRST RACE**

Course: America's Cup Course. Bearing to first mark 212°. Bearing to fourth and finish marks changed to 225°. Distance: 24.3 miles.
Wind: At start 212°, 11 knots. At finish 222°, 7 knots.

	Courageous US 26		Southern Cross KA 4	
Official Start		14:10		
Actual Start	14:10:06		14:10:08	00:02
1st Mark	14:52:32		14:53:06	00:34
2nd Mark	15:18:15		15:19:37	01:22
3rd Mark	15:38:25		15:39:58	01:33
4th Mark	16:27:30		16:30:40	03:10
5th Mark	17:25:30		17:29:35	04:05
Finish	18:22:03		18:26:57	04:54
Elapsed Time*	04:12:03		04:16:57	

Both yachts signalled their willingness to start the next day.

WEDNESDAY, SEPTEMBER 11, 1974

The second race was postponed to a later date because of lack of wind. Both yachts signalled their willingness to start the next day.

THURSDAY, SEPTEMBER 12, 1974   **SECOND RACE**

Course: America's Cup Course. Bearing to first mark 237°. Distance: 24.3 miles.
Wind: At start 237°, 11 knots. At finish 236°, 16 knots.

	Courageous US 26		Southern Cross KA 4	
Official Start		12:10		
Actual Start	12:10:09		12:10:08	00:01
1st Mark	12:55:00		12:55:34	00:34
2nd Mark	13:17:54		13:18:22	00:28
3rd Mark	13:39:54		13:40:28	00:34
4th Mark	14:24:27		14:25:23	00:56
5th Mark	14:59:55		15:00:40	00:45
Finish	15:42:37		15:43:48	01:11
Elapsed Time*	03:32:37		03:33:48	

NOTE: Both yachts finished with protest flags displayed.
Both yachts signalled their willingness to start the next day.

FRIDAY, SEPTEMBER 13, 1974

Course Signals for Race 3 were hoisted at 11:50, however the race was postponed at 12:00 because of fog.
Both yachts signalled their willingness to start the next day.

SATURDAY, SEPTEMBER 14, 1974

Race 3 was started but due to light wind neither yacht finished within the time limit which expired at 17:40.
Southern Cross requested a layover day the next day.

MONDAY, SEPTEMBER 16, 1974   **THIRD RACE**

Course: America's Cup Course. Bearing to first mark 300°. Bearing to finish mark changed to 310°. Distance: 24.3 miles.
Wind: At start 305°, 12 knots. At finish 308°, 11 knots.

	Courageous US 26		Southern Cross KA 4	
Official Start		12:10		
Actual Start	12:11:01		12:11:17	00:16
1st Mark	12:56:19		12:57:04	00:45
2nd Mark	13:18:49		13:20:14	01:25
3rd Mark	13:42:08		13:43:24	01:16
4th Mark	14:26:57		14:29:49	02:52
5th Mark	15:00:45		15:04:17	03:32
Finish	15:43:02		15:48:29	05:27
Elapsed Time*	03:33:02		03:38:29	

Both yachts signalled their willingness to start the next day.

TUESDAY, SEPTEMBER 17, 1974   **FOURTH RACE**

Course: America's Cup Course. Bearing to first mark 190°. Bearing to fourth mark changed to 215°. Distance: 24.3 miles.
Wind: At start 190°, 12 knots. At finish 214°, 12 knots.

	Courageous US 26		Southern Cross KA 4	
Official Start		12:10		
Actual Start	12:10:07		12:10:27	00:20
1st Mark	12:51:51		12:53:10	01:19
2nd Mark	13:16:26		13:18:06	01:40
3rd Mark	13:38:20		13:40:09	01:49
4th Mark	14:22:20		14:26:22	04:02
5th Mark	14:59:23		15:03:53	04:30
Finish	15:42:25		15:49:44	07:19
Elapsed Time*	03:32:25		03:39:44	

COURAGEOUS IS THE WINNER OF THE AMERICA'S CUP.

*NOTE: The Elapsed Times were taken from the times of the Official Starts.

AMERICA'S CUP RACES

RACE #2 SEPTEMBER 12, 1974   **PROTESTS**

Courageous vs Southern Cross
Southern Cross vs Courageous

FACTS

Courageous was closehauled on the starboard tack and Southern Cross was closehauled on port tack on a collision course with Courageous.

Southern Cross tacked on to starboard tack to leeward of Courageous but did not sheet in her sails.

Courageous, moving faster through the water than Southern Cross and having established a substantial overlap on Southern Cross, tacked on to port tack.

The yachts did not collide.

DECISIONS

1. **Courageous vs Southern Cross**
   The International Jury is satisfied that Southern Cross complied with the obligations laid upon her by Rule 14.

   Courageous's protest is dismissed.

2. **Southern Cross vs Courageous**
   Southern Cross did not establish to the satisfaction of the International Jury that Courageous bore away from her closehauled course while on starboard tack or that at any time Southern Cross had to bear away to keep clear of Courageous.

   Southern Cross's protest is dismissed.

INTERNATIONAL JURY
B. Croce, chairman
L. A. Sherwood
Arthur Barron

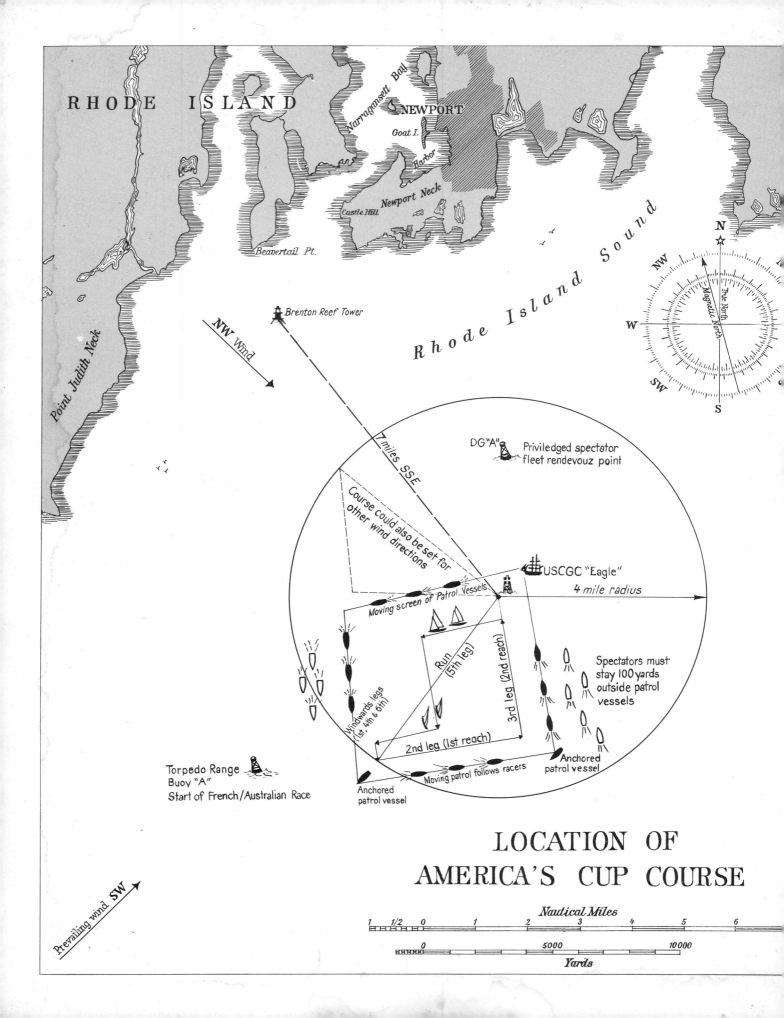

RHODE ISLAND

Narragansett Bay

NEWPORT

Goat I.

Harbor

Newport Neck

Castle Hill

Beavertail Pt.

Point Judith Neck

Rhode Island Sound

NW

N

W

E

SW

S

NW Wind

Brenton Reef Tower

7 miles SSE

Course could also be set for other wind directions

DG "A"   Priviledged spectator
           fleet rendevouz point

USCGC "Eagle"
4 mile radius

Moving screen of Patrol Vessels

Spectators must
stay 100 yards
outside patrol
vessels

Run
(5th leg)

3rd leg (2nd reach)

Windwards legs
(1st, 4th & 6th)

2nd leg (1st reach)

Moving patrol follows racers

Anchored
patrol vessel

Torpedo Range
Buoy "A"
Start of French/Australian Race

Anchored
patrol vessel

LOCATION OF
AMERICA'S CUP COURSE

Prevailing wind SW

Nautical Miles

1   1/2   0   1   2   3   4   5   6

0   5000   10000

Yards